THE CRESTLINE SERIES

VOLKSWAGEN
CARS & TRUCKS

Keith Seume

MBI Publishing
Company

First published in 2001 by MBI Publishing Company, 380 Jackson Street, Suite 200, St. Paul, MN 55101-3885 USA

MBI Publishing Company books are also available at discounts in bulk quantity for industrial or sales-promotional use. For details write to Special Sales Manager at Motorbooks International Wholesalers & Distributors, 380 Jackson Street, Suite 200, St. Paul, MN 55101-3885 USA

Library of Congress Cataloging-in-Publication Data Available
ISBN 0-7603-0982-5

Printed in the United States of America

On the front cover: Volkswagen's cars and trucks have come in all shapes and sizes over the years, including the ever-popular (top left) Golf GTI, the rare (bottom left) Hebmüller convertible, the (bottom right) stylish Samba bus, and, of course, the (top right) New Beetle.

On the back cover: Volkswagen's (top) European Polo is loved by all those who seek economy with style, while the (center) trusty Bus became a hit with the German postal service. The unusual Type 34 Karmann-Ghia (bottom) is indeed a classic .

About the Author: Keith Seume is a consultant editor for *VolksWorld* magazine and features editor for *911 & Porsche World* magazine. A former launch editor for VolksWorld magazine, he has been a moto-journalist since 1976 and specializes in Volkswagen and Porsche topics. He has also written many books on both VWs and Porsches.

Mr. Seume first drove a Volkswagen at the age of 14 and bought his first Beetle when he was 20, and has also successfully drag raced a 400-bhp turbocharged Bug. He has owned more than 40 different Volkswagens, both air- and watercooled, and he and his wife, Gwynn, own four VWs as well as a rare original Porsche 914/6 and a Porsche 911 Carrera. Mr. Seume lives in Cornwall, England.

All photos courtesy of Volkswagen AG, except where indicated otherwise.

Contents

Preface

Ask most people what car they first think of when they hear the name Volkswagen, and chances are they will say, "A Bug." Now that's hardly surprising when you consider that well over 20 million of VW's Beetle have been built in the last half century, but it doesn't really paint the whole picture.

Not long after the Beetle entered production in the latter half of the 1940s, it was joined by the VW Transporter, which was followed in the mid-1950s by the stylish Karmann-Ghia. As the world hit the 1960s, Volkswagen launched the Squareback and, a few years later, the ill-fated 411 and 412. Many people remember these models with a mixture of affection and disdain. With the 1970s arrived the Golf (or should we say Rabbit?), and today hardly a day passes without someone talking about the New Beetle. Volkswagen certainly built more than the old Bug, that's for sure.

But wait—what about the Quantum, the Dasher, and the Fox? Or the Scirocco and the Corrado? They were popular in their day and still have a big following among VW enthusiasts on both sides of the Atlantic. But these familiar models are just the tip of the iceberg. Volkswagen, you see, has been a very busy company indeed.

In this book, we have set out to show you how diverse VW's line-up has been over the years and how varied it promises to be in the future. Among the collection of photographs, you will find pictures of such models as the Saveiro, the Atlantic, the Corsa, and the Derby, vehicles which may be familiar to customers in their home markets but are practically unknown elsewhere.

In many instances, it has been difficult to even establish precisely when certain models appeared in the line-up—or when they disappeared. On a worldwide basis, Volkswagen has proved to be remarkably fluid, dropping models in one country only to launch them in another—sometimes under the same name, but more often with a new identity.

And then, you have situations in which the same name is used for two different models. For instance, in the United States everyone knows the Fox, but in Europe, the name suggests nothing more than a special-edition Polo, a model virtually unknown in North America. Or how about the Jetta? The "Golf-with-a-trunk" is sold in the United States under the Jetta name, but in Europe as the Vento, or more recently the Bora. Why? Because the Jetta never sold well outside of the United States, and Volkswagen believed a change of name might help. Future automotive historians will have every right to be confused!

The Volkswagen story is full of fascinating twists and turns, some of which would be considered far too implausible if they were written into the plot of a novel. What other company can boast that it began life under a prewar Nazi regime, was rescued from obscurity by members of the British army, and then went on to become a world leader in its field?

The story begins back in the 1920s, when Ferdinand Porsche began work on a "people's car" project for a variety of clients. NSU, Zündapp, and Wanderer were all names linked with Porsche in those far-off days and, while their plans came to nothing, the seeds were sown that led to the development of the Beetle as we know and love it today.

Along the way, an amazing variety of vehicles have carried the Volkswagen name—some good, some great, and some, well, rather uninspiring. After all, can anyone truly say the K70 was a sales success, or that it was a car that helped change the face of motoring?

These blips aside, on the whole Volkswagen has faired better than most car companies when it comes to building great cars. Today, its products are the envy of many rivals, and it is hard to imagine there ever being a future equivalent of the lackluster 411 or the K70.

I hope you enjoy this dip into the photographic files as much as I have. Here, I must once again thank my good friends at the Volkswagen archive in Germany, Eckberth von Witzleben and Dr. Bernd Wiersch. Without their assistance, this book would not have been possible. Thanks, too, to all at Volkswagen (UK) who regularly fill my mailbox with details of the latest cars—and trucks—VW has to offer. Finally, thanks as always to my wife Gwynn for keeping me chained to the Apple Mac when I would rather have been playing out in the garage!

Keith Seume
Cornwall, England
Summer, 2001

CHAPTER ONE

1920s and Early 1930s:
The Formative Years

Today, in a society in which almost every household owns at least one car, it is hard to think of what life must have been like in Germany in the 1920s. With an economy ravaged by almost five years of war, ownership of an automobile of any description was a seemingly unattainable dream for the majority of German working people. Motorcycles, pedal cycles—even horse-drawn carts—were the order of the day.

However, all this was to change with Adolf Hitler's arrival on the political scene. To be more accurate, it would have changed, had he had his way. Hitler was a small-time politician with a big following

who had a vision of Germany and its citizens climbing from the depths of deprivation and poverty to become a world-leading nation. As history proves, his means to an end were, largely, at the expense of anyone who stood in his way—including whole races of people. But, for all his evil deeds, Hitler can be thanked for one thing: His almost unflinching support for a People's Car project.

FERDINAND PORSCHE

The story of the People's Car, or *Volksauto*, begins much earlier, though. In 1875, Ferdinand Porsche, the son of a tinsmith, was born in Maffersdorf in what is

One of Ferdinand Porsche's earliest designs was the 1900 Porsche-Lohner Mixt, an intriguing vehicle which used both electric motors (mounted in the wheel hubs) and an internal-combustion engine. The gasoline engine powered generators which, in turn, provided power for the electric motors. *Porsche Archive*

Following a move to Austro-Daimler, Porsche designed the Maja, a more conventional sports-type vehicle powered by a four-cylinder gasoline engine which drove the rear wheels via a chain. *Porsche Archive*

today known as the Czech Republic. However, as much as he was pressured into following in his father's footsteps, the young Porsche had his sights set higher and soon enrolled at a technical college, where he developed a fascination with domestic electricity and that new-fangled invention, the internal-combustion engine.

However, despite his desire to learn, Porsche proved not to be an academic, instead preferring to get his hands dirty by taking a position at the United Electrical Company in Vienna. He began by doing nothing more than sweeping floors and carrying out basic maintenance work, but he soon rose to the position of head of the test department.

This promotion allowed him to develop some of his more adventurous ideas, including an electrically powered car, which featured four motors, one mounted within the hub of each wheel. Porsche pursued this design in the realization that most cars with a conventional transmission suffered performance-sapping power losses through the gearbox.

News of Ferdinand Porsche's design reached Ludwig Lohner, head of Jakob Lohner & Co., a carriage maker in Vienna. Lohner had himself been examining the possibility of building an electric vehicle and, in 1898, offered Porsche a position in his company. The young engineer was delighted to accept and immediately began

Porsche appreciated the value of competition success and entered three Maja cars in the 1909 Prinz Heinrich endurance event. All three cars won awards. The next year, Austro-Daimler cars finished first, second, and third, the leading car being driven by the young Porsche himself. *Porsche Archive*

The Sascha was Porsche's final design for Austro-Daimler. It became a very successful competition vehicle, winning Porsche much praise from his peers. *Porsche Archive*

work on building a hub-driven vehicle, which became known as the Porsche-Lohner Chaise.

A second vehicle was designed, this time using a Daimler internal-combustion engine to drive a generator to keep the onboard batteries recharged. Called the Mixt, the new design was widely acclaimed. However, by this time Porsche was beginning to hunger for a new challenge, and he left Lohner to join Austro-Daimler in 1905.

RACE TRACK CHALLENGES AND TRIUMPHS

Within a very short space of time, Porsche so impressed his new employers that he was promoted to the board of directors. His first design was for a conventional petrol-engined vehicle with a four-speed gearbox. Called the Maja, the car met with

widespread approval, despite its rather conventional layout, compared to Porsche's earlier designs. However, Porsche believed that the best way to promote this and any other vehicle was to enter it in some form of competition. As a result, three Austro-Daimlers were entered in the 1909 Prinz Heinrich Endurance Trial. All three finished in the awards. The following year, Porsche designed a new car, the Tulpenform Austro-Daimler, and entered this in the same event. Again, Austro-Daimler cars triumphed, winning no fewer than 12 of the 17 stages and the top three places overall.

Acknowledging that most cars were out of the reach of the majority of the population, Porsche soon considered designing a small car aimed at the working man. Unfortunately, Porsche's peers did not

Porsche's first break in his quest to build a mass-produced car came when he was approached by Zündapp to design a car for the masses. The result is what became known as Project No. 12, a rear-engined sedan with torsion bar suspension. *Porsche Archive*

The NSU Type 32 was the result of a brief to design an affordable family car. It represented a major step toward realizing Porsche's own dream of building a *Volksauto*. Unfortunately, an agreement between Italian manufacturer Fiat and NSU, which forbade the latter to build cars, resulted in the cancellation of the project. This vehicle survives to this day and can be viewed in the VW museum at Wolfsburg.

share his vision, feeling that such vehicles were best left to others—Austro-Daimler had, after all, built its reputation on large luxury cars. Porsche came up with one final design, the Sasha, a small sports car that impressed all who drove it. However, the company's financiers were less impressed. Porsche left in favor of a position at the German-owned Daimler factory, manufacturers of Mercedes-Benz vehicles.

Although he was employed principally to design the prestige models for which Daimler was famous—Porsche was responsible for the amazing Mercedes SSK models, for example—he could not stop thinking about his idea for a small car. Daimler's board was not so enthusiastic and, once again, Porsche was on the move. This time he found himself at Steyr, also in Vienna, where he was responsible for a small-car design and a limousine called the Austria. Both were exhibited, to much acclaim, at the 1929 Paris Motor Show, but, sadly, Steyr went into liquidation soon after. Ironically, it was Porsche's former employer, Austro-Daimler, that acquired what remained of the Steyr company.

In January 1931, Porsche left to form his own design bureau at Stuttgart, home of another previous employer, Daimler (by now known as Daimler-Benz). Among his first clients was Wanderer, which asked him to design a pair of cars for possible future production. Although neither was the small passenger vehicle that he so wanted to build, they did at least incorporate a number of Porsche's pet ideas, including torsion bar suspension.

REAR-ENGINED, AIR-COOLED *Volksauto*

Porsche's next big break came when motorcycle manufacturer Zündapp approached him with the idea of building a car for the masses. Fritz Neumeyer, head of Zündapp, firmly believed that anyone riding a motorcycle would want to step up to a car if presented the chance, with the limiting factor for most being the price. Porsche shared this thinking, and had already begun work on a concept, which was given the internal title Project No. 12. This was an unusual rear-engine car with a platform chassis, powered by an air-cooled three-cylinder radial engine.

It fitted Neumeyer's plans perfectly, and Porsche was encouraged to continue with the project. This resulted in the construction of no fewer than three prototypes, each powered, at Neumeyer's insistence, by a five-cylinder

version of Porsche's revolutionary radial engine. Unfortunately, this was to be the project's downfall, as the engines were prone to seizing, while Porsche's torsion bar suspension proved inadequate for its task.

Disillusioned by the whole situation, Zündapp pulled out of the project and left the door open for NSU, another motorcycle manufacturer, headed by Fritz von Falkenhayn. He, too, was interested in building a *Volksauto* and approached Porsche with the brief to design a small car which could be built—and hence sold—for a relatively modest sum. Project No. 32, as the design was known, reached the prototype stage in 1934. It was powered by a flat-four engine (i.e., one with the cylinders in horizontally opposed pairs), similar to airplane engines that Porsche had designed for Austro-Daimler.

Von Falkenhayn was delighted with the three vehicles that Porsche built, and the future of his *Volksauto* was looking rosy. Unfortunately, there was a cloud on the horizon, in the form of Italian manufacturer Fiat, which had forced NSU some years previous to sign an agreement which forbid it from building cars. Once again, Porsche's hopes were dashed.

While Porsche was working on Project No. 32, Adolf Hitler was appointed chancellor of Germany and head of the National Socialist (Nazi) Party. Although he was unable to drive, Hitler was passionate about cars, to the extent that he thought nothing of spending party funds on vast Mercedes-Benz tourers for his own gratification. But it was his fascination with the concept of a "car for the people" that brought him into contact with Porsche.

At the 1934 Berlin Motor Show, Hitler made a rousing speech about the need for such a people car and, shortly after, arranged a meeting with Porsche to discuss the topic. They agreed on many aspects of the design, including a low overall weight of just 650 kilograms (1,435 pounds), which would allow the use of a relatively modest 26-horsepower engine, air-cooled to reduce cost. Porsche felt such a car could be made to reach a speed of 100 kilometers per hour, but Hitler insisted that it should be able to cruise at that speed, not just reach it. After all, his new autobahns were built for high-speed travel.

Thus were sown the seeds of what would become the world's most successful car: the Volkswagen Beetle. But, as we shall see over the next few chapters, there is a lot more to Volkswagen than a buglike sedan.

CHAPTER TWO

1935–1939:
The Beetle Takes Shape

Following his meetings with Porsche, Hitler ordered the *Reichsverband der Deutschen Automobilindustrie* (RDA–the German Motor Industry Association) to work with Porsche in developing a series of prototypes. The surprise for Porsche was that the time frame was set at just 10 months, and the cost per vehicle was reduced from the originally agreed figure of 1,550 reichsmarks (the German currency of the time) to just 900 reichsmarks. Porsche felt Hitler was being unreasonable about both the time and the cost but, not wishing to argue with his benefactor, set to work with the RDA.

The association tried its utmost to stir up interest in the car industry but met little support for the project. After all, few companies shared Porsche's enthusiasm for low-cost, low-profit designs–and most resented the close relationship between Hitler and this upstart engineer.

PROTOTYPES

With little or no support forthcoming, Porsche decided to build the first prototypes himself at his own workshop in Stuttgart. However, despite his best efforts, there was no way that the cars could be ready

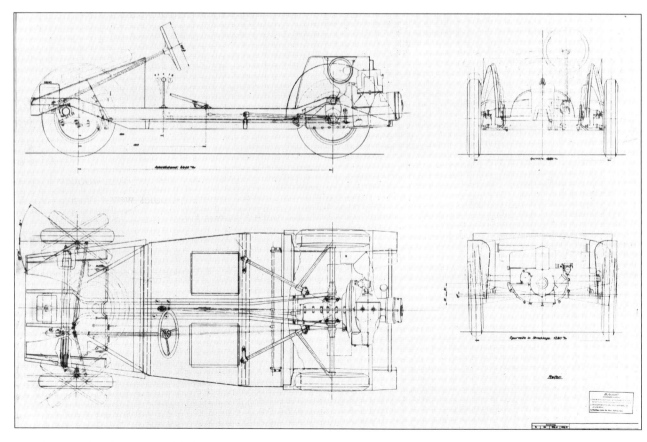

Porsche considered many possible layouts for his beloved *Volksauto*, including this 1934 design, which used unusual semi-trailing arm rear suspensions and a two-cylinder, two-stroke engine.

Porsche also felt that there was no reason why there should not be a convertible version of his *Volksauto*. This drawing, done in 1935, shows what became known as the V2 prototype.

The first prototypes to take to the road were the V1 and V2. The V1 was a sedan and can be seen here in the Black Forest behind the V2 cabriolet. This photo was taken on a Porsche family outing.

in time for the 1935 Berlin Motor Show, as Hitler had hoped. Instead, Hitler was forced to make a speech which only served to reinforce the rest of the industry's skepticism about the project. He spoke of prototypes being ready to drive by midyear, even though both he and Porsche must have known that was not possible. But who would argue with the Führer?

However, by the end of 1935, two prototypes *were* up and running, the first a sedan referred to as the V1, the second a cabriolet called the V2. Both of these vehicles were constructed with wooden frames, over which aluminum bodies were formed. One of these vehicles was fitted with a flat-twin four-stroke engine, the other with a two-cylinder two-stroke. In 1936 a series of three sedans, the VW3 models, was also built, and at least one of these cars was powered by a four-cylinder four-stroke engine.

The V1 and V2 models were the first true ancestors of the much-loved VW Beetle, but they were crudely constructed with wooden floors. The VW3 series, however, differed inasmuch as two cars (known as V3/1 and V3/2) had steel and aluminum bodies over a wooden frame, and the third (V3/3) had an all-steel body. The metal-bodied V3 cars, with their all-steel chassis, were considerably stronger than their forebears.

THE MILITARY TAKES NOTE

These first prototypes were subjected to extensive testing, not only by Porsche and his team but also by members of the RDA. The first recorded trip by a V3-series car was on July 11, 1936, when one was driven to Obersalzberg, where it was examined by Hitler. Two V3s were delivered to Berlin in August that year for examination by other Nazi Party officials, where they were received with great interest—especially by those with military leanings. Perhaps the little car could be adapted for military use, was the thought.

The V3 test program would see the tiny cars driven a total of 50,000 kilometers over all types of terrain by the most heavy-footed drivers the RDA could find. By now, all three cars had been fitted with the new four-cylinder 985-cc E-series engine, designed by Franz Reimspiess. These motors were rated at 23.5 horsepower, a little short of the projected 26 horsepower, but still sufficient to allow the V3s to reach the target 100 kilometers per hour.

The test program was not without its problems, for the cars broke down on various occasions–but then, that was what the program was all about: ironing out the inevitable problems that beset any new vehicle. The crankshafts were the biggest cause for concern. Cast by Daimler-Benz, they broke with regularity. Eventually, after the spares were used up, new forged crankshafts were made, which cured the problem once and for all.

A better view of the V2 showing the headlamp arrangement, with the two light units recessed into the front bodywork. The cars must have attracted a lot of attention out on the road, as they looked quite unlike any other passenger cars of the time.

The V2 remained in use by Ferdinand Porsche for some time and was later updated by having the headlamps relocated in the front fenders. Sadly, neither this nor the V1 survive today.

The VW3 was a series of three prototypes, of which V3/1 and V3/2 had steel and aluminium bodies formed over a wooden frame, while the third, referred to as the V3/3, had an all-steel body shell and chassis.

By the end of the program, the V3s had collectively covered a total of 150,000 kilometers and met with the approval of Porsche and the RDA. But that was not the end of the matter. Based on the experience gained with the V3 series, the RDA now wished to produce yet more prototypes. The new cars were to be called the VW30—a reference to the number of examples built. Of these, 29 were constructed by Daimler-Benz but the other—the first of the series—was actually built from scratch in Porsche's own garage!

The VW30 was a considerable improvement on the V3 models, with smoother lines and a far higher standard of finish. Powered by a development of the V3's 985-cc engine, the VW30 was to be the subject of yet more extensive testing by the RDA, this time over some 80,000 kilometers per vehicle—an incredible distance in the days when many roads in Germany were little better than dirt tracks.

The test drivers were all recruited from within the SS, Hitler's feared security troops. Each test driver was sworn to secrecy over the project, and about the only requirement was that they be able to drive. In some instances, this ability came into question, and more than a few had to be taught the correct way to drive a car. This may seem crazy today, but it is important to remember that, at the time, few private individuals regularly drove a car, let alone owned one.

Two V3 sedans parked outside the Porsche villa during the extensive test program that saw the cars driven a total of 50,000 kilometers (31,000 miles) over all kinds of terrain. This took place late in 1936.

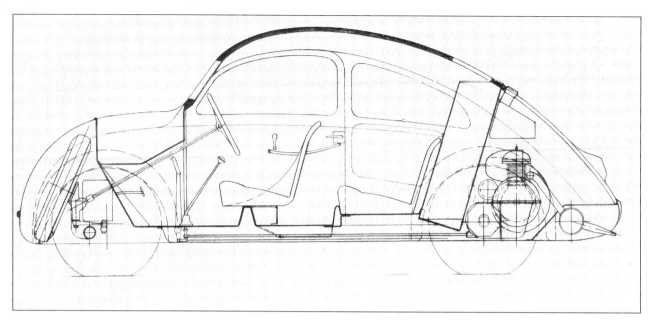

Another design drawing, this time marked up as a four-seater sedan powered by a transversely mounted engine—another idea that progressed no further than the drawing board.

The V3 series was superseded by the VW30, of which 30 examples were built for test purposes. The VW30 is on the left, the V3 on the right. Rearward vision was limited to what could be seen out through the louvers.

The test program was successfully completed, following the inevitable mishaps which befall any such intensive driving. Cars crashed, cars broke down, and some drivers were fired, but overall the Porsche team and the RDA were pleased with the results, which cleared the way for the next series of prototypes, the VW303 models, to be built.

The VW303s were identifiably the first true Beetles, although that name wouldn't be used for another decade, and then only in a colloquial fashion.

Of the 30 VW30s built, 29 of them were assembled by Daimler-Benz. The remaining one was built from scratch in Porsche's own garage.

The VW30 was a relatively small sedan, but shared the same wheelbase of 2,400 millimeters (94.5 inches) with the final production version of the VW Beetle. Note the semaphore turn signals in the front quarter-panels and the tiny trunk lid.

Work on the VW303s, descendants of the VW30 models and sporting a similar chassis, began in 1938. However, in response to the lessons learned from the VW30, the body design was quite different, with reducing production costs and increasing the rigidity the primary objectives. Under the guidance of Erwin Komenda, Porsche's chief designer, new plans were drawn up, and, following the construction of a pair of wooden mock-ups, three steel bodies were made by local coach builder Reutter.

The new design incorporated front-hinged doors, unlike the rear-hinged "suicide" doors of the VW30s and all previous prototypes. For the first time, the design included running boards, which kept the sides of the vehicle clean. Bumpers for front and rear protection were fitted somewhat reluctantly, as they significantly added to the production costs of the vehicle.

Of the three VW303s, one was a regular sedan, another a sunroof (rag-top) model, while the third was a full cabriolet. They were scheduled to be completed in time for the 1938 Berlin Motor Show, at which Hitler was due to announce their launch. However,

The VW30s were driven in all conditions, including busy city centers, in order to discover any weaknesses in the design. Its body shape forms quite a contrast with the magnificent tourers in the background.

A team of army test drivers was chosen to drive each of the VW30s over a distance of some 80,000 kilometers (50,000 miles). Several cars suffered major mechanical failures but, overall, they held up well to the best and worst efforts of the driving team.

The interior of the VW30s was Spartan, with simple tubular-framed seats covered in coarse woolen cloth. The front seats tilted forward to give access to the rear. Note the rear-hinged "suicide" doors.

that deadline soon proved unworkable, so a new date was set: May 26, 1938–Ascension Day. This was the date set for the ceremonial laying of the cornerstone at the new factory, purpose-built to produce the new Volkswagen, near Fallersleben, close to what is now known as Wolfsburg. At the Berlin Motor Show, Hitler surprised everyone by referring to the car as the KdF-Wagen–the "Strength Through Joy Car." The name is from the political KdF (*Kraft durch Freude*) movement in Germany, which had been set up by the Nazis to look after the welfare of the working people.

KDF-WAGEN MAKES ITS DEBUT

The cornerstone-laying ceremony marked the first public appearance of the KdF-Wagen, and it was

met with great interest. Hitler was driven around the factory site and, subsequently, to the local railway station in the back seat of the cabriolet VW303. This is reputed to be the car that is on display in the Volkswagen museum at Wolfsburg.

The Porsche team pressed on with development work, which led to the construction of 30 new VW38 models, each with a redesigned chassis. While they were being built, the order was increased to 44 examples. However, not all were destined to be what we now refer to as Beetles—at least four were used as the basis for prototype military vehicles, while three

Wherever the VW30s went, they attracted enormous attention, and there appeared to be no attempts made to keep them away from the public eye. From this angle, through the windshield, you can see how poor the rearward visibility was.

Test driver Herbert Kaes took his VW30 everywhere, and it clearly made a hit with the girls! The rear-mounted engine gave the car excellent traction, even in soft snow, while air-cooling meant there was no radiator to freeze.

Kaes poses next to a VW30 prior to the cars being broken up at the end of the test program. In the background, stripped body shells await destruction.

Porsche envisioned his little car being used as the base for all sorts of vehicles, including this light delivery van.

more were used as the basis for the famous Type 64 Berlin-Rome sports cars. This all took place toward the very end of 1938.

At the same time, 50 VW39 prototypes were ordered, to be built by July of the following year. However, it became clear that several of these never made it into sedan form. Once again, many of the chassis were diverted toward military projects, including prototypes for the Type 84 Kübelwagen and the Types 128 and 166 *Schwimmwagen*.

In an amazing publicity campaign designed to raise public interest in the project, the VW38 cars were driven all over Germany. A savings scheme was introduced whereby, for five reichsmarks a week,

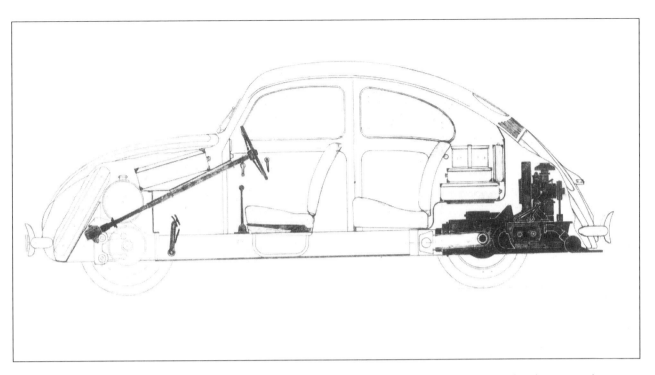

The *Volksauto*, or People's Car, project was officially known as the Type 60. It wasn't until May 1938 that the name KdF-Wagen was coined by Adolf Hitler, much to Porsche's annoyance.

Following the success of the VW30 program, all efforts were turned to the next phase of the project. Work began on building a wooden mock-up to assess the styling —note, for example, the shape of the front fenders around the headlamps.

The first of the new cars, called the VW303, is examined by members of Porsche's team at his workshops. The body shell was made by the local Reutter coachworks. The 1938 VW303s were the first true Beetles.

Left: On May 26, 1938, three VW303s were used at the cornerstone-laying ceremony at the KdF factory. Of these, one was a sedan (not shown), another a rag-top (left), and the third a cabriolet (right).

workers could buy a savings stamp. When they had saved up the equivalent of 990 reichsmarks, they could exchange the savings stamps for a new KdF-Wagen. At least, that was the theory, but in reality, no worker ever took delivery of a car, resulting in a lengthy postwar legal battle between Volkswagen and representatives of the prewar savers.

In February 1939, the DAF (*Deutschen Arbeitsfront–* German Workers' Party), which headed the KdF-Wagen program, invited a number of international journalists to sample the little air-cooled car on a lengthy test route that included several kilometers of Hitler's new autobahn. The outcome was almost universal praise for Porsche's sedan, with only the engine noise a source of criticism.

Although the car had now been seen in public on several occasions and the world's press allowed to drive finished examples, there was still no sign of the KdF-Wagen becoming available to the public. War in Europe was looming, and attention was being diverted toward military projects rather than mass production of a passenger car. The factory had not been completed, either, further slowing things down.

In September 1939, war was declared between Germany and Poland. The KdF-Wagen program was put on the back burner. Suddenly, the development of a cheap military vehicle was of greater importance. The Kübelwagen was about to steal the limelight.

Hitler was extremely pleased with what he saw that day and seemed satisfied with his ride in the cabriolet from the event to the nearby railroad station. Note the high standard of finish on the fenders.

The three VW303 models made an attractive line-up at the ceremony. However, the process of building the next series of prototypes had already begun.

Thirty more prototypes were due to be built, and were to be called the VW38 (they were built in 1938, hence the name). The order was increased to 44, although not all were completed as sedans—some chassis were destined to be used as the basis for military prototypes.

The KdF-Wagen was put on display to the world at the 1939 Berlin Motor Show, where it was greeted with tremendous interest.

Porsche was rarely photographed smiling, but he must have been pleased with the success of his project. Here he rests against a rag-top sunroof VW38.

The dashboard of the prewar cars was little different from those of the first postwar Beetles. There was even provision for a radio, even though relatively few contemporary cars were so equipped.

In August 1939, a group of VW39 prototypes went on a nationwide tour to promote the KdF-Wagen. The route took them up into the Alps and over the Grossglockner Pass.

Needless to say, wherever the VW39s went, they drew crowds of interested onlookers. Herbert Kaes (to the right, with hands in his pockets) probably covered more miles than any other test driver at the wheel of virtually all Porsche's prototypes.

Every opportunity was taken to promote the KdF-Wagen. A series of specially commissioned publicity photographs showed the KdF-Wagen in a number of typically German settings.

Not all prototypes survived the rigorous testing unscathed. This particular car was severely damaged in what appears to have been a rollover accident. A combination of excessive speed, a sharp corner, and swing-axle rear suspension, perhaps?

Hermann Goering, head of the Lüftwaffe (German air force), tries the back seat of a cabriolet for size. Each of the main Nazi Party leaders was given a KdF-Wagen for their own use, but it's unknown how many chose to drive them in preference to their usual Mercedes limousines!

In 1939, a group of journalists was given the opportunity to drive the KdF-Wagen on an extended test route which took them past the site of the new factory. Here they are pausing to take in the view of the *KdF-Stadt* in the distance.

At least one pickup truck version of the KdF-Wagen was built, but none survive. This aerial view shows the tiny hatch built into the pickup bed to allow access to the engine.

The test drive took in all kinds of roads, from new autobahns to small, dusty tracks. Most journalists were impressed with what they saw (and drove), with only a few criticizing the little car for its excessive engine noise.

Three streamlined cars, referred to as the Type 64, were built to contest the proposed 1939 Berlin-Rome road race. However, the outbreak of war caused the event to be canceled, so they were used largely as runabouts by the Porsche team.

The Type 64s were aerodynamically very efficient and should have been highly competitive, had the race taken place. One car survives to this day, but the other two were destroyed after the war.

KdF-Wagens were exhibited all over Germany in an effort to encourage people to join the savings scheme, by which they could buy a stamp every week until they had saved enough to buy a car. Sadly, not one of the savers ever had the opportunity to collect their KdF-Wagen.

1938–1945:
War and Peace

By the outbreak of World War II, the final form of the Type 60–the in-house designation of the KdF-Wagen–had been decided. But there were other projects afoot within the Porsche design studio, principally a military version of the People's Car, a project discussed as early as five years previous.

On April 11, 1934, a meeting was held at the Berlin offices of the German Transport Ministry to consider the suitability of the proposed *Volksauto* for adaptation into a military vehicle. Representatives of the Reichs Chancellery demanded that any such vehicle be capable of carrying three soldiers equipped with a machine gun and ammunition. It would be almost a year before further progress was made, when Porsche, the RDA, and military officials met again to discuss specifications in greater detail.

The separate chassis of the VW30, with its self-contained drivetrain and suspension, lent itself admirably to the idea of fitting lightweight bodywork and turning it into a useful off-road vehicle for the military.

In December 1937, this rather crude-looking vehicle was shown to military officials to gauge their opinion. It consisted of little more than four fenders and two tiny seats, with a large machine gun mounted on the front. This was, however, enough to demonstrate the potential offered by the VW30 chassis.

In 1938, two more prototypes were built, this being the second. It was more sophisticated than its predecessors and included a third pair of "helper" wheels alongside the driver and passenger to prevent the vehicle from bottoming out over rough terrain.

Clearly based on the VW38 (one of the KdF-Wagen prototypes), this one-off was completed in November 1938. It was designed by Franz Reimspiess and had the in-house design code of Type 62.

By now, the project was far enough advanced to seek Hitler's approval. The Führer showed great interest in all of Porsche's work, and he found his military project particularly fascinating.

Near the end of 1937, while the VW30 prototypes were undergoing their extensive test program, one car was removed from its test duties and stripped of its body. This is almost certainly the body shell seen cut in two lengthwise for exhibition purposes. The bare chassis was then shown to various officials in Berlin to demonstrate its suitability for use as a platform for a military vehicle.

A VW30 chassis, possibly the same one, was then equipped with rudimentary bodywork, which consisted of little more than four fenders and an engine cover, two crude seats, and the mounting for

Late in 1939, what can be considered the first version of the final Type 62 design was built. It was starting to look more like a purpose-built military vehicle rather than a mocked-up chassis or modified sedan. However, there was still a long way to go.

The chassis of the VW38 prototype was far stronger than that of the old VW30 and required little or no modification for use in a military role.

In 1939, just months before the outbreak of war, another prototype was constructed. It was more angular but had no doors and only a very crude folding top. However, it showed potential and led to the development of the final Type 82 design.

In the eyes of Hitler's party faithful, Dr. Porsche (seen here on the right) could do no wrong. His designs for military hardware ranged from the Kübelwagen up to the mighty Tiger tank.

a light machine gun. To aid cross-country ability (remember, this was the chassis of a road-going car), a third pair of wheels was attached, one wheel on each side of the chassis, midway between the front and rear axles. The idea behind this was to lift the center of the vehicle over any obstacle that might otherwise have caused it to bottom out.

This vehicle was shown to the military officers in December 1937, and shortly after that, Porsche was presented with a revised *Wehrmacht* (military) specification. The overall weight was not to exceed 950 kilograms (2,100 pounds), which included the combined weight of three soldiers and their equipment, taken to be 400 kilograms (884 pounds). That only left 550 kilograms (1,215 pounds) for the vehicle and, given that a bare VW30 chassis weighed approximately 400 kilograms (884 pounds) itself, it was clear the body had to be basic at best.

Early in 1938, a second prototype was built, and it was a considerable improvement over the first.

Despite the outbreak of war, the opportunity was still taken to display the finished Kübelwagen and KdF-Wagen to the public. This was probably the only time that a Kübel was seen with shiny tires.

Kübelwagen production began in earnest in 1940—in fact, the very first entry in the factory ledger is for a Type 82. The KdF-Wagen sedan had been sidelined to make way for the assembly of military vehicles.

The Kübelwagen was a simple vehicle to build, the completed bodies arriving from the Berlin-based Ambi-Budd company ready for installation on the completed chassis. Ambi-Budd was a part American-owned company.

A third followed shortly after. The *Stuka*, as this prototype was nicknamed, proved to be very agile over rough ground. It offered better protection from the elements, and still featured the third pair of "helper" wheels. The man responsible for its design, Franz Xaver Reimspiess, completed the assignment (in-house reference Type 62) in record time.

Toward the end of the year, another prototype was constructed. It was clearly based on the VW38 sedan, with its rounded bodywork and an integral windshield.

By December 1940, no fewer than 1,000 Type 82s had been built—cause for a small celebration. Once the photograph was taken, it was back to the production lines for the hard-pressed workers.

The Kübelwagen excelled in thick, glutinous mud. Much of the fighting on the Russian front took place in such conditions, and *Wehrmacht* troops were quick to appreciate the Type 82's capabilities.

Gone were the side-mounted helper wheels, but there was now a hood-mounted spare wheel. However, there were still no doors. Canvas roll-up side covers and a very crude folding roof were the only protection from the elements. The vehicle was first shown to the military in November 1938 and then displayed in public at the Vienna Motor Show early the following year.

Despite the positive response from most quarters, the HWA (*Heeres Waffen Amt*–the German Army Weapons Office) was somewhat concerned about the vehicle's ground clearance and its lack of four-wheel drive. However, Porsche's own test drivers, headed by Herbert Kaes, were soon able to demonstrate that the Type 62 was sufficiently

By way of contrast, the Kübelwagen also excelled in the desert campaigns in North Africa. Its air-cooled engine meant that it didn't suffer from overheating, as did so many water-cooled army vehicles.

The Type 82's light weight made it ideal for use in soft sand. Field Marshal Rommel claimed he owed his life to a Kübelwagen after his driver accidentally strayed into a minefield. The low weight of the Kübel meant that it did not trigger any land mines—unlike a heavier vehicle following behind.

The Kübelwagen was so light that it could easily be tipped on its side for ease of maintenance—or to bail out any water!

agile to allow it to outperform many better-equipped vehicles.

Nevertheless, Porsche's team recognized short-comings, and, in January 1939, yet another design was drawn up. This bore a far closer resemblance to the final Kübelwagen, with its angular bodywork, but it still had no doors and only a simple folding roof. The matter of insufficient ground clearance was addressed by fitting large 18-inch-diameter wheels, with tall 5.0x18 tires. Compared to the stock KdF-Wagen's 16-inch wheels and 4.50x6 tires, this gave the Type 62 up to 40 millimeters (1.6 inches) more ground clearance.

Mechanically, the Type 62 was virtually identical to the KdF-Wagen, with the same 985-cc engine that produced just 23.5 horsepower. However, there was one difference: the design of the exhaust system. All previous prototypes had been criticized for their lack of ground clearance at the rear, due to the low-slung muffler based on that of the sedan. The new system consisted of two mufflers mounted high up, along-side the clutch bell housing, with two separate tailpipes directing exhaust gases to the rear.

WORLD WAR II

In the fall of 1939, a further development of this angular design was built, this time with four steel doors and a more sophisticated roof with better protection for the occupants. By the time the prototype appeared, war had been declared against Poland. Porsche's design was almost finalized, and speed was of the essence. But there were still some problem areas with which the *Wehrmacht* was unhappy.

Ground clearance remained a bone of contention, despite the use of the larger-diameter wheels and tires. Porsche eventually addressed this problem by incorporating reduction gearboxes on the ends of each axle, used in conjunction with modified front stub-axle assemblies. This increased the ground clearance by 30 millimeters (1.2 inches) and reduced the gear ratios slightly. The lower gear ratios helped the off-road capabilities and allowed the vehicle to trickle along at a modest three miles per hour in first gear, enabling the vehicle to be driven alongside a marching soldier. This was another of the *Wehrmacht's* requirements.

The Type 128 amphibious vehicle project came about as a result of a request from the *Waffen SS* for a lightweight vehicle using a KdF-Wagen engine mounted in a motorcycle frame. Porsche had other ideas, and suggested a purpose-built vehicle capable of driving on the road or wading through water.

Not all test sessions went according to plan! Here, the prototype Type 128 gets a helping hand out of the water, much to the amusement of the onlookers.

The new improved design, called the Type 82, became the mainstay of the German army throughout World War II. Series production began in 1940, and the very first entry in the hand-written production record in the factory archives in Wolfsburg reads: Type 82 Kübelwagen. So much for building a car for the working people. The Kübelwagen was not the only military variant to be built, for Porsche also built an amphibious military vehicle called the Type 166 *Schwimmwagen*. The roots of this project can be traced back as far as the mid-1930s, when designer Hannes

The Type 128 design was revised still further following encouraging results gained by the first prototype. A rear-mounted propeller driven off the crankshaft pushed the vehicle along when in the water, while an ingenious four-wheel drive system gave it outstanding off-road abilities on land.

Hitler, seen here on the left, was delighted with the progress made with the Type 128 and gave it his full support. Heinrich Himmler, Hitler's top lieutenant (right center), seems equally interested.

The final outcome of the amphibious vehicle project was the Type 166 *Schwimmwagen*. Note the propeller, which could be swung up out of the way when the vehicle was driven on the road.

The Type 166 was an extremely impressive vehicle, both in and out of the water. It was capable of attacking very steep slopes, thanks to short front and rear overhangs.

Trippel drew up plans for an amphibious military vehicle. In 1939, he was actually commissioned by the German Army to develop his ideas further with a view of putting such a vehicle into production.

However, Trippel was not alone in his thinking. Porsche also saw the potential for such a vehicle and, late in 1939, began sketching out ideas for a version of the Kübelwagen that could be driven on dry land and in water. The impetus for the project came from the *Waffen SS*, which asked Porsche if it would be possible to fit a KdF-Wagen engine into a motorcycle frame for use as an all-terrain vehicle.

It was normal practice to enter the water slowly to prevent a bow wave from flooding the *Schwimmwagen*. Great fun was had by all during testing and it is easy to forget, when looking at photographs such as this, that a bitter war was raging throughout Europe.

Generous ground clearance meant that the Type 166 could be driven over all kinds of obstacles without fear of grounding. Here Herbert Kaes puts a prototype through its paces in the forest.

Porsche did not see the sense in that idea and instead began work on an altogether more sophisticated machine. The result was referred to as the Type 128, the first prototype of which appeared in 1940. He also worked on a four-wheel drive system (Types 86 and 87), the technology of which would ultimately be incorporated in the *Schwimmwagen* project.

AN AMPHIBIOUS KÜBELWAGEN

The Type 128 first took to the water in the fire pond at the KdF factory, where, although far from

This British army officer looks pretty happy to be taken out for a cruise on the Mittelland Canal in a *Schwimmwagen* at the end of the war. The vehicle was steered in the water by the front wheels.

The Kübelwagen was converted for all kinds of uses during the war and many prototypes were built to test different ideas. This tracked version was principally intended for use in snow or thick mud.

An alternative track arrangement, which was possibly meant for use in soft sand. What its on-road manners were like is a matter for conjecture!

Look closely and you'll see a Kübelwagen hiding under this disguise. This unusual vehicle was built to help train tank drivers. It could also be used as a decoy to fool enemy aircraft.

perfect, it showed potential. The main problem lay with the shape of the body, which was little different from that of the Kübelwagen from which it was derived. The second version was much improved in this respect, with its boat-shaped body providing better performance and maneuverability in the water. By the end of September 1940, several examples of the revised Type 128 had been built and extensively tested in the Max-Eyth-See, a lake close to Stuttgart.

Mechanically, the Type 128 was virtually identical to the Type 82, with the exception of an ingenious four-wheel drive system. Drive to the front wheels was taken from the nose of the centrally mounted gearbox to a differential located between the front axle torsion tubes. A rear-mounted propeller was driven off the crankshaft by a coupling that allowed it to be pivoted up and out of the way when the vehicle was being driven on dry land.

The Type 128 proved a success in almost every respect and, as a consequence, Porsche was given the go-ahead to develop the concept still further—the result was the Type 166, the *Schwimmwagen*, first seen in late 1942. This was similar to the Type 128 but had a shorter wheelbase (2,000 millimeters as opposed to 2,400 or 80 inches as opposed to 94.5 inches) and the body was narrower. To cope with the power-sapping all-wheel-drive system, Porsche increased the engine size to 1,131 cc, thus raising the power output to 25 horsepower, a modest but worthwhile improvement. This same engine was also installed in the Kübelwagen in 1943, which further improved this already versatile machine.

The *Schwimmwagen* became another of Porsche's success stories, for it earned itself tremendous respect from all who relied on it for transportation in arduous conditions. But its story doesn't end there. Porsche also developed a four-wheel-drive version of the KdF-Wagen, the Type 877. Commonly, but incorrectly, referred to as the Type 87, this vehicle became known as the *Kommandeurwagen*. It was intended for use by higher-ranking officers in the battlefield, but relatively few were built between 1942 and 1944. The Type 877 was joined by the Type 82E, a KdF-Wagen body on a two-wheel-drive Kübelwagen chassis. (The Type 87 designation really refers to an all-wheel-drive Kübelwagen prototype.)

But what of the KdF-Wagen itself all this time? Sadly, the German people never got their People's Car, for all efforts were redirected toward military vehicle production. Some 336,638 people had paid a weekly sum of five reichsmarks to buy a savings stamp toward the purchase of a KdF-Wagen, but not one ever received a car in exchange for a completed savings books. That isn't to say, however, that KdF-Wagens weren't produced in wartime. Some 630 sedans and 13 cabriolets were built between July 11, 1941, when production officially began, and August 7, 1944, when the pressures of war brought production to a close. Compare those figures, though, with the total Kübelwagen production of 50,000 and over 14,000 *Schwimmwagens*, and it's easy to see where the priorities lay.

Yet another variation on the Type 82 theme was this fire pump. By the addition of a water pump driven off the crankshaft, the Kübel could be transformed into a useful emergency fire tender.

A close-up of the fire tender's engine and pump arrangement. Note the heavy-duty air filter fitted to the engine for use in dusty conditions.

The KdF-Wagen continued in limited production throughout the war, with every example built being put to use by Nazi Party officials and their supporters. Sadly, not one single member of the German public ever got behind the wheel of their own car, despite a national savings scheme that allowed them to collect stamps up to the value of a new vehicle.

The post must get through! Converting a Kübelwagen into a simple box van meant that the wartime postal service could still make deliveries, regardless of conditions.

Another quiet celebration as the first KdF-Wagens are readied for delivery to their new owners in 1941.

The Type 877 was a four-wheel drive version of the KdF-Wagen sedan for use by officers in the front line. It was built between 1942 and 1944 in relatively small numbers. A similar two-wheel-drive version was called the Type 82E.

Like the Kübelwagen, the KdF-Wagen was also cut down and converted into a delivery van for the *Reichspost* (the German wartime post office). The raised suspension suggests the use of a Kübelwagen-type chassis.

An ambulance version was also envisaged, which again used Kübelwagen running gear for increased ground clearance. Note the externally mounted semaphore turn signals on the front quarter-panels.

The rear door of the ambulance swung wide open to allow the stretcher to be fed through a small slot, where it poked through into the cabin alongside the driver. Not the most sophisticated of conversions, by any means!

Toward the end of the war, Germany experienced severe gasoline shortages. This led to a number of alternative fuels being tried out. This Type 82E was converted to a wood-burner. Somehow, one can't imagine the performance being that great!

The factory took direct hits from Allied bombers in 1944, resulting in widespread damage to the production lines. Here, the body of a *Schwimmwagen* hangs precariously from the collapsed ceiling.

CHAPTER FOUR

1945–1959:
Years of Growth

On the night of April 8, 1944, the KdF-Wagen factory received several direct hits during a massive air raid. The factory was chosen as a target for Allied bombers, not only because of its Kübelwagen production lines, but also because part of the works had been turned over to aircraft manufacture.

Some 2,000 bombs were dropped during the raid and, as can be imagined, damage was extensive. To add further to the confusion, an American bomber crashed onto the factory, causing yet more damage. These two events effectively brought production to a halt, although workers struggled amid the ruins to produce a few more vehicles before production finally ceased on August 7, 1944.

By this stage of the war, it was clear that all was lost, even if Hitler refused to accept that fact. Efforts were made to conceal some of the machinery used at the factory in the vain hope that the Reich might rise again, but it was a pointless exercise. On April 10 and 11, 1945, American troops eventually appeared on the doorstep at the *KdF-Stadt*, little knowing what lay within. The town did not appear on any of the military maps, so its discovery came as something of a surprise to many of the troops.

The Nazis in control at the factory, anxious to escape the clutches of the Allied troops, left the workers to fend for themselves. Never before had so many people been so happy to be taken prisoner by soldiers

The first Beetles assembled by the British army were rather crude, being built largely from parts found among the ruins of the factory. The increased ride height was a consequence of using Kübelwagen running gear.

With an order from British military headquarters for no less than 20,000 units, the early production lines were kept busy. Working conditions were poor, and there were frequent stoppages due to a shortage of parts.

A line of freshly built Beetles ready for delivery to the British army. These early cars were essentially replicas of the wartime Type 82E models, with their Kübelwagen drivetrain and KdF-Wagen body shells. Their official designation was Type 2.

who just days before were considered the enemy. The reason for this was that close behind the American troops was the Russian army, and every German feared what reprisals the Communists might take.

When Germany was partitioned in 1945, with the nation and its resources split between the British, Americans, Russians, and French, the *KdF-Stadt* fell under British jurisdiction. Ah, but hold on: There was now no KdF movement–it had disappeared the day the Nazis capitulated–so, strictly speaking, there could be no *KdF-Stadt*, or KdF-Wagen, for that matter. In May that year, following a meeting of the local

This neat pickup, with its matching trailer, was built to deliver cars locally. It was converted from a regular sedan by simply cutting off the original bodywork behind the doors and substituting a one-off pickup bed.

Probably the most famous of all postwar specials built at the factory in the 1940s was the so-called Radclyffe Roadster. Its ultimate fate is unknown, but its design lived on in the form of the later Hebmüller roadster.

This crude transporter was built using the drivetrain of a Beetle mounted on a substantial chassis. It was used for carrying parts around the factory grounds and is considered by many to be the true forefather of the VW Transporter.

town council and representatives of the MilGov (the Allied-controlled military government), the decision was made to rename the town Wolfsburg, after the local castle, Schloss Wolfsburg, which had been the family seat of Count von Schulenburg before the war.

Under the command of MilGov, a British officer, Col. Michael McEvoy of the Royal Electrical and Mechanical Engineers (REME), was sent to the region to assess what could be salvaged and put to use by the British army. When he arrived at Wolfsburg, he discovered among the ruins the remains of half-built vehicles, along with a considerable amount of engineering equipment. McEvoy felt that the factory had potential, not only as a workshop to repair army vehicles, but also—just maybe—to put the VW back into production, albeit on a limited basis. This was not the first contact McEvoy had with the Volkswagen, as the car came to be called once

Maj. Ivan Hirst was more aware than most of the importance of selling the Beetle abroad to increase the Volkswagen factory's chance of survival. A number of special models were built for display at trade shows in Germany. Note the external chrome horns and the unique hubcaps.

more. Before the war, he had worked at Mercedes, where he had driven a prototype version. If anyone could appreciate its potential, he could.

VOLKSWAGEN GMBH

In August 1945, McEvoy placed Maj. Ivan Hirst, also of the British REME regiment, in command of the works, and it was this modest but capable officer who was largely responsible for the rebirth of the VW. To begin with, Hirst looked at the possibility of building Kübelwagens for use by the Forces of Occupation, but it turned out vital presses had been destroyed in an air raid on the Berlin-based Ambi-Budd company, which was responsible for making the bodies. Instead, Hirst assembled a couple of sedans, using the chassis and drivetrain of a

The factory's experimental workshops made several attempts at building a Beetle cabriolet in the late 1940s, but few were really successful. Note the tiny two-piece rear window and externally mounted semaphore turn signals on this early example.

This second version had its semaphores mounted flush with the front quarter-panel for a more finished look. The main problem that beset these early prototypes was the windshield surrounds flexing, causing the glass to break.

The first Karmann-built cabriolet dates back to late 1946. It differed from production models by having the semaphores in the front quarters—series-built cabriolets came with them located behind the doors.

Kübelwagen and the KdF-Wagen bodies. Volkswagen GmbH was born.

One of these hastily assembled vehicles was delivered to MilGov headquarters, where it was received with great enthusiasm—so much so that Hirst was sent an order for no fewer than 20,000 of them! The Volkswagen Beetle legend was about to begin. Hirst's team began assembly of what were essentially Type 82E models for use by the army and, soon after, orders began to pour in from the French, American, and even Soviet forces.

With production now under way on a fairly organized basis, despite a shortage of raw materials for the production lines and coal for the power station, Ivan Hirst was approached by Colonel McEvoy with the idea of building a VW-based racing car.

This is an intriguing photograph, for it is clearly of a Beetle built on a high-riding Kübelwagen chassis, yet it was finished to a very high standard and was fitted with Export body trim. It also featured a later (possibly 1950) body. Note, too, the unique hinged rear side windows.

In January 1949, VW boss Heinz Nordhoff sent Dutch importer Ben Pon (on the left) to the United States to see if he could sell Volkswagens there. One car was shipped across the Atlantic, but Pon's efforts were in vain. The car was sold to cover his costs and he returned home with an empty order book.

Hirst thought the idea rather silly under the circumstances, but it did set him thinking about alternative body styles to the regular sedan. He set Rudolph Ringel, head of the experimental workshop at Wolfsburg, the task of designing a two-seat roadster. Just one example was built and duly presented to Col. Charles Radclyffe, Hirst's commanding officer. Henceforth, the car was known colloquially as the Radclyffe Roadster.

This attractive vehicle was used regularly throughout the summer months by Radclyffe until it was severely damaged one day by his driver. As a consequence, a new chassis was fitted, and the vehicle was

returned to service. Its ultimate fate is unknown, but it was most likely scrapped, along with many other prototype vehicles.

In 1946, Hirst received a visit from Wilhelm Karmann, head of the coach-building firm of the same name, with a view to acquiring chassis on which to build a cabriolet version of the Volkswagen. Josef Hebmüller and Sons, another coach builder, made a similar request. Karmann's proposal was for a full four-seat convertible, while Hebmüller preferred the idea of a two-seater, not unlike the design of the Radclyffe Roadster.

Unfortunately, neither company was able to progress far with its projects, due to a lack of cars to

By 1950, the Beetle had developed from a crude, hand-assembled vehicle into a well-finished automobile, fit for sale around the world. Export models came with body trim, chromed bumpers and hubcaps, as well as hydraulic brakes.

In January 1951, the infamous "crotch coolers" made their appearance in the front quarter-panels. These simple ventilation flaps were intended to provide fresh air to the interior, but tended to give the occupants a draft where it was least appreciated!

One of the very first prototype Transporters built early in 1949. Note the rather poor finish to the bodywork and the single windshield wiper. This was just one of a series of preproduction models built to test the soundness of the design.

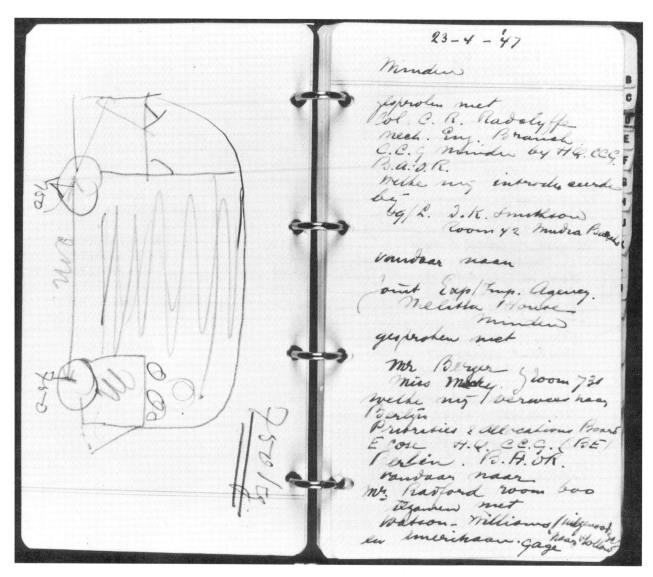

At a meeting in April 1947, Ben Pon sketched out his ideas for a light delivery vehicle built around Volkswagen components. His design called for a rear-mounted engine and the driving seat over the front wheels to leave plenty of load space in the center of the vehicle.

convert. Karmann was eventually given a car—the 10,000th to roll off the production line—in November 1946 and, soon after, built two prototypes. But that was as far as things went for another two years because the factory could not spare any more cars.

Hebmüller just beat Karmann into production, its two-seat roadsters first appearing in June 1949. The first Karmann cabriolets rolled off the assembly line at Osnabrück in September 1949, reaching a production level of six cars per day by December that year. Karmann's production rates increased dramatically the following year, with the 1,000th car being completed by April.

Sadly, Hebmüller did not have a happy future ahead, for a massive fire raged through the factory in July 1949, temporarily halting production. Although work started again within four weeks, Hebmüller never quite recovered, finally closing its doors in 1952, the final 14 two-seat Beetles being built for Hebmüller by the rival Karmann factory.

In 1948, by which time Beetle production was going strong, Ivan Hirst appointed Heinz Nordhoff general director of Volkswagen, and in 1949 the factory was finally signed back over to the German people. The era of British management was finally at an end, but a new era was about to begin.

Another prototype, this time dressed up to show how the proposed Transporter might look as a delivery vehicle for a private business. The license plate reads Type 29, the official factory designation for the Transporter.

On November 12, 1949, Heinz Nordhoff hosted a press briefing to launch the new Transporter. It received very favorable reviews in the contemporary press, especially as many rival products were so crude.

Under Nordhoff, the company went from strength to strength—he more than anyone else realized the importance of two things: exports and service. He knew that, even though there was a huge demand from the domestic market for low-cost transport, it was vital for Volkswagen to win orders from abroad. He also knew that there was no point in selling cars without spare parts and a service network to keep them on the road.

In January 1949, Nordhoff sent a car to the United States in an effort to drum up interest in the product. It was left to an enthusiastic Dutchman by

Another prototype, possibly number 6 or 7, looked particularly smart in its attractive two-tone paint scheme.

The top-of-the-line Deluxe buses were known as Sambas and featured windows in the roof, a full-length sunroof, and extra body trim. This is a 1955 model, with semaphore turn signals.

Built around 1951, this is a prototype of the factory-built ambulance. Ambulances and other emergency vehicles formed part of the transporter line-up from the earliest days of production.

Built by German conversion specialists Westfalia, this drop-side wide-body pickup dates back to 1957. Westfalia was one of the few independent specialists to be sanctioned by Volkswagen.

the name of Ben Pon to try to convince the Americans of its worth. If anyone could do it, it would be Pon. Back in 1947, he bought six cars from the factory to sell in his homeland, despite strong anti-German feelings among the Dutch people. Sadly, despite his enthusiasm, Pon could not convince the skeptical Americans and he returned home disillusioned.

VW ENTERS THE U.S. MARKET

It would be a further two years before Nordhoff was able to win over the U.S. market, following the appointment of a distributor, Max Hoffman of Chicago. Hoffman fared better, selling no fewer than 330 cars in 1950 alone.

By this time, the product had improved considerably, with export models now having hydraulic brakes and attractive brightwork on the body. The domestic, or Standard, models retained the cable braking system and austere bodywork.

But we mustn't forget Ben Pon, for it is he who is often credited with another little idea to put Volkswagen at the top of a new market: a light delivery vehicle. Even while Ivan Hirst had been in control, there had been talk of building a Beetle-based van, but early prototypes proved unsuccessful. In 1947, Pon sketched out his idea for a rear-engined, cab-forward delivery vehicle that could be based on Volkswagen components.

The first official mention of such a vehicle was made in a memorandum dated November 11, 1948. Within months, the first prototypes were built. One year

later, in November 1949, Nordhoff proudly showed the world's press the very first Volkswagen Transporter.

Powered by the same 25-horsepower, 1,131-cc engine as the sedan, the VW Transporter went on sale in March 1950. The first to be sold, chassis number 000014, was delivered to Autohaus Fleischauer in Cologne and sold to the 4711 perfume company. The first example to be exported (chassis number 000032) was supplied to Ben Pon in Holland in July that year, while the first to be sent overseas was chassis number 000591, which went to Volkswagen's own plant at Sao Paolo, Brazil.

Production of the Type 2, as the Transporter was designated, continued at Wolfsburg until 1956, by which time it was evident that there simply wasn't the capacity at the factory to cope with both Beetle and Transporter assembly. A new plant was opened in Hannover especially for the Type 2, and production of VW trucks continues there today.

The VW Transporter spawned several variants, including the Kombi, a multipurpose vehicle with removable rear seats that could be transformed from a passenger vehicle to a delivery truck in minutes, as well as an ambulance, a fire truck, a pickup, and a camper van. The list is almost endless, such was the versatility of the design.

THE KARMANN-GHIA

But the Beetle and the Transporter weren't the only products to carry the Volkswagen name in the 1950s. Alongside the sedan and the cabriolet, a new

This one-off vehicle was built by Westfalia to show how a VW Transporter might be converted for use by the German postal service (*Deutsche Bündespost*). Unfortunately, the *Bündespost* felt the vehicle was too small to be of practical use.

face appeared in 1953 when Karmann, following lengthy discussions with Heinz Nordhoff, showed the prototype of a very stylish sports coupe. Designed by the Italian Ghia styling studio, it was called the VW Karmann-Ghia. It was a hit from the start, appealing to anyone with an eye for the unusual. However, to begin with, Nordhoff was skeptical about its viability, as there was little spare capacity at the factory for producing the necessary chassis and mechanical components.

In America, the Karmann-Ghia coupe was enthusiastically accepted, despite its somewhat lackluster performance. Late in 1957, it was joined by an equally stylish cabriolet model. The future was suddenly looking very rosy indeed for Volkswagen—or was it?

Heinz Nordhoff seemed convinced that the Beetle would see the company through the next decade, and possibly beyond. Many changes were made to both its mechanical specification and appearance—the rear window, for example, changed from two small windows to a larger oval one in 1953, and then again to an even larger one in August 1957—in an effort to keep ahead of the opposition. Others around him were not so convinced and encouraged him to consider a replacement for the Beetle. In reality, Nordhoff had already been thinking about the future. At his instigation, by the end of the 1950s several prototypes had been built, with the aim of one day replacing the Type 1 with an altogether more modern vehicle. The new decade would see many changes and new faces in the Volkswagen line-up.

No, your eyes are not deceiving you. This Transporter really is running on a railroad track. Built by Beilhack in 1954, it was intended for use as a railcar. A turntable mechanism allowed the vehicle to be lifted and turned to drive back down the line.

This specially built Transporter was used by the *Österreichische Post-und-Telefon Verwaltung* (Austrian Post and Telephone Administration).

In 1953, the first Beetle began to undergo some improvements to make it more appealing, especially on the export market. Vent wings (quarterlights) in the door glass improved ventilation, while extra chrome trim around the windows added some sparkle. The dashboard was also redesigned, as were the taillights.

The big news for the 1954 model year was the introduction of the oval window model. The new rear window resulted in far better rearward vision for the driver, making the car safer to drive on roads that were becoming busier each year. A new 36-horsepower engine also meant better performance.

Rag-tops, as the full-length fold-back sunroofs were often known, especially in the United States, were a popular option in the 1950s. Today, rag-top Beetles are much sought after.

Despite their relative lack of power, Beetles soon became recognized as potential rally winners—especially in Scandinavia, where VWs competed very successfully in some of the toughest events in the world.

Both Heinz Nordhoff of Volkswagen and Wilhelm Karmann of the coach-building company of the same name dreamed of building a sports car in the early 1950s. The end result of this shared dream was the Karmann-Ghia, of which this is the 1953 prototype.

Viewed from the rear, the prototype was not too far removed from the final production version. However, the stylists had still not settled on the design of the taillights, deck lid, or bumpers.

From the very beginning, there were plans to build a cabriolet version of the Karmann-Ghia. This prototype, also built in 1953, shows a different design of front fender and bumper. Note the somewhat heavy-looking vent window (quarter-light).

By 1954, the styling had almost been finalized, but still the taillights were not quite to everyone's taste—nor were the bumpers.

Sergio Sartorelli is the man generally credited with the final design of the Ghia—he was the head of styling at the Turin design studio. This photograph was taken at the 1955 press launch of the Ghia coupe.

Work on the Karmann-Ghia cabriolet continued alongside the coupe, although the open version was not released until September 1957. Surely, this is one of the most elegant Volkswagens ever built.

Early Ghias (prior to August 1959) are referred to as low-light models—a reference to the height of the headlamps in the front fenders. Later cars had redesigned fenders which located the lamps a few inches higher.

A removable hardtop was considered for the Ghia cabriolet, but this idea never made it past the prototype stage.

The Karmann-built Beetle cabriolet continued to sell extremely well throughout the 1950s, especially in the United States where there was a huge market for convertibles.

As far as Heinz Nordhoff was concerned, quality control was of great importance if the Beetle was to continue to sell well on the world market. Here a factory inspector checks the paintwork of a freshly sprayed body shell for defects.

In August 1957, the Beetle underwent another major restyle, with the arrival of the first of the so-called big-window models. These had not only a greatly increased rear window area, but also a completely new dashboard design.

The rag-top sunroof model continued in production alongside the regular sedan and cabriolet. European Beetles still came with semaphore turn signals right up until 1960, even though U.S.-spec cars had been fitted with flashing turn signals since 1955.

From the side, it is hard to see how much the Beetle had changed since it went into production at the end of 1945. But there had been many improvements: rear window, bumpers, vent windows, wheels, dashboard and, under the skin, a new engine. However, this was only the beginning, for the next decade would see even bigger changes.

Throughout the late 1940s and the 1950s, several companies chose to use a VW Beetle as a starting point from which to create something altogether more stylish. Hebmüller was among the first to appreciate the potential offered by the Bug, starting back in June 1949 with its two-seat roadster. Compare this with the Radclyffe Roadster shown earlier in this chapter.

Hebmüller also built the Type 18A model for use by the police. It was essentially a cut-down sedan, without doors for easy access. These were replaced by crude, roll-back canvas flaps.

Even with the top up, there was little in the way of worthwhile weather protection for the occupants. Note the ropes across the door openings to prevent the passengers from falling out while going around corners!

Johannes Beeskow was the man responsible for the styling of the Rometsch. Based on a contemporary Beetle, the stylish Rometsch was available as either a practical coupe or this elegant roadster. It was first seen in 1950 at the Berlin Motor Show, with production starting the following year.

In 1957, another stylist, Bert Lawrence, designed this new Rometsch—again available as a coupe or cabriolet—which had clearly been influenced by styling trends in the United States.

Built as a prototype for the *Deutsche Bundespost*, this Beetle-based delivery van used what appeared to be cabriolet doors and a similar squared-off windshield surround. Sadly, it never went into production, and it is not known how many examples were built.

Unbelievably, this woody is based on a Beetle! You don't need to look too hard to find the clues—the wheels and their distinctive hubcaps are a surefire giveaway. This is just one of the many one-offs built by enterprising companies in the 1940s and 1950s. *Keith Seume*

The EA48 was one of many prototypes built by Volkswagen as possible alternatives to the Beetle which, by the mid-1950s, was no longer the cheap transport it used to be. Powered by a 700-cc (some reports suggest 800-cc) two-cylinder engine mounted in the front, it featured advanced MacPherson-strut suspension. Today, it is on view in the new Autostadt museum at Wolfsburg.

CHAPTER FIVE

1960–1969:
Years of Change

With the arrival of the new decade, Volkswagen displayed greater confidence than ever before. Its products were selling well across the world, including strong sales in the United States, where the Beetle was the number one choice among purchasers of small cars. The Microbus, as the Kombi model was known in the United States, proved to be very popular, as it was the first of what we today call MPVs—multipurpose vehicles—which can do double duty as family runabouts or weekday workhorses.

Under Heinz Nordhoff's command, it seemed Volkswagen could do no wrong. In an effort to keep up with demand, production at Wolfsburg was stepped up to over 4,000 units per day, yet even this was not enough to cope with the huge demand. Many dealers were forced to quote a five-month waiting list for delivery of a new Beetle, while most rivals could meet their demand in a matter of days.

Detractors accused Volkswagen of being too reliant on the excellent sales of just one model, and

As Volkswagen entered the new decade, the trusty VW Transporter remained a strong seller on both sides of the Atlantic. Customers loved the versatility of models such as the Kombi (Microbus).

The Volkswagen Camper was the number one choice around the world for many families traveling on a budget. Literally dozens of companies specialized in camper conversions in America alone.

Volkswagen always listed emergency vehicles among its Type 2 line-up. This fire truck was produced in 1962—the WOB license plate suggests it was a factory-owned vehicle. (WOB stands for Wolfsburg.)

analysts were quick to point out the folly of having too narrow a product range. Despite appearances to the contrary, however, Nordhoff was one step ahead. The first sign that something was afoot was when the Beetle received a new engine and gearbox in August 1960 for the 1961 model. The engine was based on the unit fitted to the Type 2 (Transporter) models the previous year, and with a 13 percent power increase, it made a good car even better.

But that was not all Nordhoff had up his sleeve, for in September 1961, Volkswagen launched the Type 3 range. This consisted of a two-door Notchback sedan and a two-door wagon, officially called the Variant but forever referred to in the United States as the Squareback. These two vehicles were vastly superior to the Beetle in so many ways that they appealed

to a whole new market. With a clever redesign of the engine (by now enlarged to 1,498 cc, as used in the revised Type 2), the Type 3 models featured trunks back and front, giving them enormous luggage capacity compared to rival products.

The Type 3 arrived at just the right time, for the Beetle's sales had taken an 8 percent downturn, at a time when car sales in Germany were *up* by 10 percent. The Beetle was suddenly being viewed as underpowered and lacking in refinement. Other inexpensive

A right-hand-drive 1965 ambulance—note the external two-tone horns, the blue emergency light, and the smaller St. John's light above the windshield.

cars, such as Britain's Mini, were seen to be modern and exciting–the Beetle was the same old car which had been around for years. VW dealers welcomed the Type 3s with open arms for, at last, they had something new to show their customers.

The Type 3 sedan and wagon were joined at their Frankfurt Motor Show debut by the interestingly styled Type 34 Karmann-Ghia–a radically different model from the previous Type 1–based vehicles. With its so-called "razor-edged" styling (a reference to the crisp lines of the Sergio Sartorelli design), the Type 34 created quite a stir when it was first shown to the public. Its styling was clearly aimed at the U.S. market, where the angular appearance was supposed to suggest a European look.

Interestingly, at the same time these three new models were put on display, two others almost stole the limelight: the Type 3 and Type 34 cabriolets. Examples of both cars were displayed at Frankfurt but, despite the publication of promotional brochures showing them ready for sale, neither model made it into production. Engineers at Wolfsburg decided at a late stage that they lacked rigidity, while marketing personnel felt they were not economically viable products. It was a costly and embarrassing exercise for Volkswagen–something it could have done without.

One of the more interesting vehicles to join the VW line-up was a small delivery vehicle that was designed principally for use by the German post

In August 1960, Volkswagen announced big changes to its Beetle, with a new engine and transmission. Other improvements included the use of flashing turn signals in all markets (available on U.S.-specification cars since 1955).

The German postal service used right-hand-drive Beetles for deliveries so that the driver could step straight out onto the sidewalk. This is a 1961 model. Note the black-painted bumpers and wheel rims.

In 1962, further modifications were made to the Beetle, including new taillight clusters with separate yellow turn signal lenses on European models. American-spec cars used all-red lenses.

In 1964, the so-called Export (Deluxe) models were offered with a steel wind-back sunroof in place of the former sliding cloth rag-top version.

office (*Deutsche Bundespost*). Officially designated the Type 147, the dumpy vehicle was christened by the public as the *Fridolin*, a name that has remained in popular use to this day. It was based on the floorpan of the Karmann-Ghia, which itself used a widened Beetle chassis. Many other components, such as lights and trim (such as it was) were raided from the Type 2 and 3 parts bins.

In August 1965, the Notchback and Squarebacks were joined by the stylish Fastback, a two-door four-seater coupe which some people referred to as a poor man's Porsche. (It's amazing what a few pints of beer and a vivid imagination can do.) With this trio of more sophisticated models, which included the ever-green Beetle and the versatile Type 2, Volkswagen's line-up looked more impressive than ever. By September 1965, 10 million vehicles had been built at Wolfsburg since the end of the war. But there was yet more to come—some good, some bad.

INTERNATIONAL ACQUISITIONS

In the mid-1960s, several major events occurred which would have an effect on the future of the VW line-up. To begin with, in January 1965, Volkswagen acquired a controlling interest in the long-established Auto Union company. In November of the following year, it acquired the Brazilian Auto Union operation run by Vemag, Brazil's third-largest vehicle manufacturer. In November 1967, VW then began production of the 1,200-cc Beetle at a new plant in Puebla, Mexico. Clearly, despite a sluggish start to the decade, Volkswagen was in a buoyant mood.

The Beetle saw many changes during this period, the first major one being the option of a 1,300-cc engine for 1965, followed by the Type 2–derived 1,500-cc engine for 1967. European 1500s even came with disc front brakes, although models destined for the United States never benefited from this obvious safety advantage. Then, in 1968, the Beetle was given a whole new look, with heavier bumpers, upright headlamps from the Type 3 range and redesigned engine lid, along with a host of less-obvious modifications. Many of

American-specification 1967s were only fitted with drum front brakes, for some obscure reason. Perhaps Americans didn't drive as fast as their European counterparts!

The most desirable of all Beetles remained the cabriolet. Built by Karmann, the cabriolet was hugely popular in North America. Extra strengthening under the rocker panels kept the body shell rigid.

Considered by many to be one of the best Beetles ever made, the European 1500 model came with a new, more powerful engine and was also equipped with front disc brakes.

The Beetle underwent a major restyle for the 1968 model year, with a new shorter deck lid and heavier "Euro" bumpers. The taillights were also enlarged to meet U.S. safety regulations.

In September 1961, the all-new Type 3 range was launched. The Variant (known as the Squareback in the United States) was an extremely useful wagon, which had an enormous amount of luggage space.

VW introduced the Type 3 sedan, or Notchback, at the same time as the Squareback. With a trunk in front and another at the rear, it was a very practical car. This model was never officially offered in the United States. Notchbacks proved popular with rally drivers, especially in Scandinavia.

Alongside the Squareback and Notchback at the 1961 Frankfurt Motor Show was this attractive Type 3 Cabriolet. It was all set to go into production (even the sales brochures had been printed) when the decision was made to axe it from the line-up. Shame.

these changes were dictated by impending safety legislation in the United States, while others were simply intended to give the Beetle a new lease on life.

The Type 2 also received a revamp for the 1968 model year, with the introduction of the so-called "bay-window" Transporter. This new model featured a large one-piece windshield and a much-improved rear suspension system that finally did away with the reduction gearboxes on each axle, a design feature that can be traced back to the wartime Kübelwagen. With an up-rated engine, this revised Type 2 was more pleasurable to drive, and it soon became a sales success.

The year 1968 was an important one for Volkswagen in many ways. In March, the Australian VW factory launched its Beach and Bush Car, a simple,

no-frills off-road vehicle largely intended for recreational or agricultural use. Then, in April, Heinz Nordhoff, the man largely responsible for VW's postwar success story, passed away at the age of 69. His successor, Kurt Lotz, proved to be a controversial leader, with many of the company's less-successful cars being launched during his term at the top.

In August, the all-new Type 4 411 model was released, a heavyweight luxury sedan powered by a new 1,700-cc air-cooled engine. It marked a radical departure from conventional Volkswagen design, as it featured MacPherson-strut front suspension and a body/chassis of unitary construction. Fuel injection was also offered, along with a fully automatic transmission, a feature also offered on the Type 3 but

The Fastback joined the Type 3 range in 1965. All the Type 3s were redesigned in 1968, with heavier "Euro" bumpers and bigger taillights. The hood was also reshaped to give extra luggage space.

By 1966, the Type 3 had already sold one million. This was clearly a cause for celebration at Wolfsburg.

never on the Beetle (although a so-called "stick shift" semi-automatic Beetle was available for those who preferred not to use a clutch).

History proved the Type 4 to be something of a failure, despite its being improved several times over the years. There were two- and four-door models, Squareback variants, and even a prototype Notchback, but nothing seemed able to save the overweight, underpowered 411. Even the launch of the much-improved 412, with its larger and more powerful 1,800-cc engine, couldn't save the Type 4's reputation. It quietly slipped from the product range in 1974.

But there were other vehicles that were equally intriguing, such as the Type 181–popularly known in the United States as the Thing or the Trekker. Originally designed as a military vehicle, somewhat in the vein of the original Type 82 Kübelwagen, the Thing proved to be very popular in the United States and in countries with a climate where its lack of weatherproofing and minimal creature comforts were less of a drawback. The Type 181 went into production in August 1969 and was built until 1976 in Wolfsburg, with production continuing in Mexico (where it was known as the Safari) for another couple of years. Its main drawback as far as a civilian market was concerned was the price. Built to exacting military standards, the 181 was simply too costly by the time it appeared in the show room.

The Type 3 was a very clever design, its rear-mounted engine hidden away under the floor. Vents in the tops of the rear fenders provided air for the cooling system.

THE 914 AND 914/6

One of the more unlikely vehicles to join the VW line-up in the late 1960s was the VW-Porsche 914 sports car. The result of a collaboration between two of Germany's most important car manufacturers, the 914 was intended to offer an upmarket alternative to the rest of the otherwise strait-laced Volkswagen family. Porsche regarded it as an entry-level model in its range, aimed at introducing new customers to the delights of Porsche ownership. Two versions were on offer: One powered by the four-cylinder engine used in the Type 4 range, the other—called the 914/6—was fitted with the 2-liter flat-six engine of the Porsche 911T coupe.

The 914 was not a massive success, suffering from something of an identity crisis. In Europe, the VW-powered models were sold as VW-Porsches and offered by Volkswagen dealers, while the six-cylinder model was sold through Porsche agencies. In

America, a whole new marketing operation was set up, with all models being referred to as Porsches, yet sold through VWoA's newly formed Porsche & Audi division. Eventually, after just under 119,000 sales, the 914 quietly slipped from the range in 1975, though Porsche had already axed the 914/6 at the end of 1971, as it had not proved profitable.

So, the 1960s were clearly a time of change at Volkswagen, with several new vehicles introduced—not all of them successful—and numerous upgrades on some familiar models. But the poor reception the Type 4 received was indicative of the problem faced by Volkswagen: No longer could the German giant guarantee that its products would be an instant sales success. Times were changing and the public was starting to demand more from its cars. To maintain its place in the market—let alone expand—Volkswagen was going to have to do some serious thinking.

The Type 3 was widely used by the German police. Here, four Squarebacks keep a *Polizei* Beetle and Transporter company.

Throughout the life of the Type 1–based Karmann-Ghia, several proposals were made for a replacement. This design study dates back to 1962.

Although the Karmann-Ghia may have looked like a high-performance sports car, under the skin it was almost pure Beetle. The only major difference was that the floorpan was made slightly wider to aid rigidity.

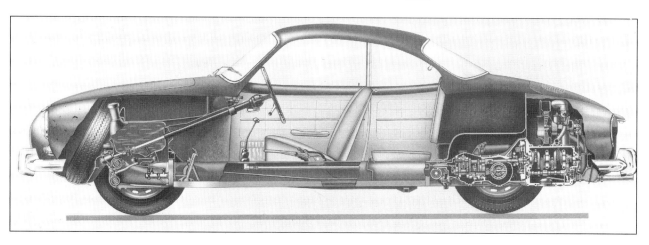

The Type 34—more commonly known as the Type 3 Ghia, or Razor Edge, in deference to its styling—was launched at the 1961 Frankfurt Motor Show alongside the new Type 3 range.

The Razor Edge Ghia was intended to appeal to the U.S. market, with styling that was supposed to be typically European. For many customers, though, its appearance was simply too unusual.

The new Karmann-Ghia was originally going to be offered as a cabriolet, but, like the Type 3 convertible, the model was dropped before it went into full-scale production. High cost and poor rigidity were said to be the reasons.

The Type 147 was better known as the *Fridolin*—it was a light delivery vehicle built on the floorpan of the Type 1 Karmann-Ghia. It became the mainstay of the *Deutsche Bündespost* (German post office). Note the sliding side doors.

In August 1967, the Type 2 took on a whole new look, with a wider one-piece windshield and more modern styling. However, it had lost none of the old model's versatility.

There were plenty of changes under the skin, too, with a new rear suspension system giving a superior ride. Then, in 1971, disc brakes would replace the original drum front brakes.

The new Transporter was soon adopted by the postal service in Germany. This particular example was registered to the telephone department of the *Deutsche Bundespost*.

The second-generation Type 2 was available in a wide variety of body styles, one of the more practical being the double-cab (or crew cab, as it was also known). It offered all the advantages of a pickup with seating for five.

Officially referred to as the Type 197, this Australian-built utility vehicle was known as the Country Buggy or Beach and Bush car. Launched in March 1968, it was a simple design, cheap to build, and cheap to maintain.

Even with the top up, there was precious little weather protection for the occupants of the Country Buggy. Note the Beetle headlights.

In 1968, Volkswagen embarked on another fateful project, the Type 4. Launched as the VW 411, the Type 4 was overweight and underpowered. It was the first air-cooled production model to have four doors.

The front end of the Type 4 was dominated by the large headlamps and panoramic windshield. The front trunk was cavernous, and there was plenty of interior space, too.

Although the 411 was a slow seller, the factory still thought it worth celebrating the 10,000th example to roll off the production lines.

Volkswagen even considered building a Notchback 411, referred to as the EA142. The prototype, built in 1966, can be seen on display at the VW museum in Wolfsburg.

The Type 4 range received a boost late in 1973 with the launch of the 412. Despite the improved styling and more powerful engine, the Type 4 was destined to be one of Volkswagen's less successful ventures.

The 411 and 412's fastback styling would have lent itself to a hatchback design with luggage space above the engine. Instead, VW provided them with basic storage space behind the seats, accessible only from within.

The Type 4 Variant was far more practical, with considerable luggage space at the back and a huge trunk in front. This is a fire department vehicle, complete with flashing blue light and radio equipment.

The Type 181 was originally developed for military use, with Beetle-based mechanics and a wider Karmann-Ghia floorpan. It was sold to the general public as the Trekker or, in the United States, as the Thing. It was too expensive to be a major success.

One of the greatest things about the Trekker, or the Thing, is that you can remove all the doors and fold down the windshield in a matter of minutes to make a fun, go-anywhere buggy. Note the Type 2 taillights.

Once again, the *Deutsche Bündespost* adopted the Trekker for use in rural areas where road conditions wouldn't allow a more conventional vehicle to venture. The basic top kept out the worst weather.

In Mexico, a special edition of the Trekker was offered, known as the Acapulco. It came complete with Surrey top and brightly colored seats, making it just the thing for cruising to the beach on a hot summer's day!

Although production of the Type 181 ceased in Germany in 1976, it continued to be assembled in Mexico for another couple of years. It was sold as the Safari.

The EA160 was the prototype for a four-door Type 3 Notchback. It never made it into production, and the sole example still survives in the VW Museum.

Called the EA97, this prototype almost made it into production as a replacement for the Type 3. However, such plans were rejected, and the tooling was sent to South America where, in revised form, it went into production as the first Brasilia.

Truly a Volkswagen like no other, this 1965 Karmann-designed and -built model was seen as a possible replacement for the Karmann-Ghia. It never made it past the prototype stage.

Another view of the Karmann prototype. Note that each side of the car has a different treatment of the vents in the rear fenders. What a shame this never made it into production.

The EA97/1 was a study for a Beetle replacement. Work started on the project as long ago as 1957 and continued until 1963. However, the arrival of the Type 3 effectively put an end to this idea.

From the front, you can clearly see the link with the Beetle. Unfortunately, the EA97/1 had lost all the Beetle's charm, looking overweight and overstyled. Not one of VW's better efforts.

This Ghia design for a Beetle replacement was part of the long-running EA53 project, which lasted from 1954 to 1961.

The EA266, with its water-cooled engine mounted below the rear seats, was one of the most talked-about design projects. About 50 different examples were built of this Porsche-designed prototype before the project was axed by Rudolph Leiding because of spiraling costs.

The Rovomobil was not a factory design, but built by enthusiasts in East Germany. It had an impressive "cd" figure of just 0.24. It, too, resides in the Volkswagen Museum at Wolfsburg.

CHAPTER SIX

1970–1979:
The Winds of Change

The 1970s saw an amazing change in Volkswagen's line-up. For instance, not all VW products were to be air-cooled, and soon the Beetle would no longer be the number one vehicle in the range.

With the acquisition of NSU in 1969, Volkswagen inherited a somewhat poorly conceived four-door sedan, powered by a front-mounted, water-cooled engine. Not only was the engine at the wrong end, according to VW lore, but it drove the front wheels, via a transaxle unit. This was, indeed,

a radical departure from what had become established as the VW norm.

The NSU-designed, VW-built sedan was called the K70 and, sadly, its name has become synonymous with a low point in Volkswagen's history. Put simply, the K70 was a disaster in just about all respects.

The problems began with the engine itself. It was a 1,700-cc unit which produced an honest 75 horsepower (90- and 100-horsepower versions were also offered) but

Volkswagen's first attempt at building a water-cooled car came in the form of the 1970 VW K70 (right, shown here next to a VW 412 [Type 4]). The K70 was a disappointment, having a voracious thirst for gas.

The EA276 was an experimental front-wheel-drive compact that began life with an air-cooled engine in the front. The EA276 was eventually developed into what became known as the Golf/Rabbit.

The Karmann-Ghia continued in production in its original form, the Type 34 model having been dropped due to poor sales. The Ghia eventually disappeared from the VW line-up in 1974.

proved to be unreliable and, occasionally, prone to overheating. Next was the matter of the styling. The K70 was the most literal translation of the "three-box" term applied to car styling that you could imagine. Square and anonymous, the K70 made even the VW Type 4 look stylish. And then there were the aerodynamics. The K70's disappointing gas mileage was largely the result of a dreadful "Cd" figure (the coefficient of drag—a measure of the car's ability to cut through the air) which was measured at 0.51, when even the old Beetle's was only 0.44. Not a promising start.

But worst of all from Volkswagen's standpoint was the fact that the K70 cost too much to build, and once sold, it cost too much in warranty problems. Add all this to the poor sales of the Type 4

The ESVW of 1971 was one of Volkswagen's many prototypes designed to explore new safety features. Although the vehicle was never intended to go into production, its styling was a foretaste of future models.

In August 1970, the Beetle got a completely new look with the arrival of the 1302 and 1302S models, with their MacPherson-strut front suspensions and new, more powerful engines. *Volkswagen (UK)*

The new models came with either 1300 or 1600 engines, the latter being fitted to the 1302S version. In all markets except the United States, the 1302S came with front disc brakes.

In August 1972, the 1302 was replaced by the new 1303 range. The curved windshield was a styling first for the Beetle—some people loved it, but many hated this new look. *Volkswagen (UK)*

From the rear, the 1302 and 1303 Beetles can be distinguished from the more basic models by the extra vents in the deck lid—and the new badging, of course. New large taillights were used on 1303s. *Volkswagen (UK)*

and a gradual slowing down of the European economy, and you have the recipe for a time of hardship for Volkswagen.

The Beetle continued to sell in surprising numbers and, on February 17, 1972, it reached the ultimate sales milestone by becoming the biggest selling car of all time. As Beetle number 15,007,034 rolled off the production line, it ousted Ford's legendary Model T from the number one position–and there was plenty of life left in the old Bug yet.

There were, however, changes made in an effort to keep the Beetle at the top. For 1971, the first of the Super Beetles was produced. Officially known as the 1302 and 1302S models, the redesigned Beetles were powered by 1,300-cc and 1,600-cc engines. These engines featured new cylinder heads with individual inlet ports for each cylinder, as first seen on the Type 3 range.

Of greater technical interest, however, is the front suspension: For the first time in the Beetle's

history, Ferdinand Porsche's favored torsion bars were no longer used. In their place was a new MacPherson strut setup, similar to that used on the Type 4. At the back, an independent rear suspension (IRS) system was used, first seen on the stick shift models from September 1967 and U.S.-specification models from August 1968.

The Super Beetles did not really give the Beetle line-up the boost it needed, for the design was still

Ghost view of the 1303S (note the front disc brakes) shows the sophisticated suspension system used on these models. Handling was much improved.

Every Beetle that left the factory was thoroughly examined by a team of inspectors. Here a 1303 is having its wheel alignment checked prior to delivery.

By the mid-1970s Volkswagen was aware that the Beetle was losing some of its appeal. To combat this, the company dreamed up new ways of icing the cake—this was the GT Beetle, a European special with a 1,600-cc engine, disc brakes, and swing-axle rear suspension. *Volkswagen (UK)*

essentially out-of-date. Compared to its rivals, the Beetle lacked performance and, perhaps above all, space. In August 1972, the Super Beetles were redesigned with a large, curved windshield and deep padded dashboard. It was an effort to give the almost 40-year-old design a fresh look, but it didn't work, and the Beetle's sales continued to slowly decline. The new models, the 1303 and 1303S, were dropped without ceremony from the line-up at the end of July 1975.

The K70 wasn't the only water-cooled vehicle with which Volkswagen was involved in the very early 1970s. Through its Audi sister operation, water-cooled sedans were being produced, and they quickly established an excellent reputation. In June 1968, Audi launched the 100 model, a full-sized sedan ready to take on the lower end of the Mercedes mar-

ket. This was joined in 1972 by the 80, a midsized sedan, which was almost launched with a fastback body style under the Volkswagen name. Unfortunately, the prototype mid-engined EA266 pushed that idea to one side.

VW PASSAT/AUDI 80

However, the seeds had been clearly sown and, in 1973, Volkswagen announced that it would be marketing its own version of the Audi 80 under the name Passat. The front-engined, water-cooled sedan, known in the United States as the Dasher , was a worthy car, but its immediate success was affected by the first of the world oil crises. This, however, was only the beginning. Volkswagen shocked its critics by announcing the arrival of two all-new water-cooled

Another popular limited-edition model was the Jeans Beetle of 1974, with its denim-trimmed interior and bright yellow or red paintwork. Beetle production in Europe was soon to cease and such models helped keep interest alive. *Volkswagen (UK)*

VWs: the Golf and the Scirocco (don't forget, the K70 had been, in reality, an NSU). The Scirocco was an attractive sports coupe´, while the Golf was a little hatchback sedan that came to be known as the Rabbit in the United States and Caribe south of the border. Presumably, the original name was thought to be too confusing to Americans. Rabbit was meant to imply sprightly performance and fun, two attributes the Golf—sorry, Rabbit—had in abundance.

Styled by Giorgetto Giugiaro at his Ital Design studio, these two cars were based on the same front-wheel-drive floorpan and powered by transversely mounted four-cylinder engines that were largely derived from the Audi unit used in the 80 and 100 models. The task of assembling the stylish Scirocco was given to old associates Karmann in Osnabrück, which still built the Beetle cabriolet for Volkswagen.

The Scirocco was chosen as the first to be launched for the following reason: Volkswagen was placing a lot of importance on the success of the Golf and, therefore, felt it better to release the lower-

In 1973, Volkswagen launched the Passat (known as the Dasher in the United States), a midsized fastback sedan based on Audi's 80 model. Unfortunately, its launch coincided with the first of the world's oil crises.

The Dasher Wagon was the North American equivalent of the European Passat Variant which, in turn, was called the Passat Estate in Britain. One car, so many names . . .
Volkswagen (UK)

All aboard! Lüfthansa (German national airline) publicity photograph shows a U.S.-specification Passat (Dasher) on a pallet ready for transport to North America. This was a publicity stunt, for most cars were sent by sea.

volume Scirocco first in order to iron out any possible production or technical problems. The last thing VW wanted was for a possible successor to the Beetle to get off on the wrong foot.

The Scirocco was launched in March 1974 and was well received. It was followed in July that year by the three-door (actually two doors and a hatchback) Golf, which was then joined one month later by a five-door version. There were three engine options, each an overhead-camshaft design. The Scirocco was powered by a 70-horsepower, 1,471-cc unit, first used in the Passat; a high-compression 85-horsepower version of this; or by a puny 1,093-cc engine, which produced a modest 50 horsepower. The Golf came with

either this 1.1-liter or the 70-horsepower, 1.5-liter unit, depending on the model.

After the joy of seeing the new models launched, the workers at Wolfsburg soon had cause to shed a tear, for on July 1, 1974, the very last Beetle to be built at the original VW factory came off the assembly line in order to make way for the new Golf. Assembly continued at VW's other plants at Emden and Hannover (as well as in South America), and Beetle body shells would still be produced at Wolfsburg for the foreseeable future.

There was another new product just around the corner, too, in the form of a larger Volkswagen commercial vehicle, known as the LT. First produced in

The Passat Variant (also called Estate and Wagon) was available in a variety of specifications. This is a Passat LX, which came with a sunroof, alloy wheels, and a radio cassette unit. *Volkswagen (UK)*

In the early days, the Passat was built alongside the Beetle at Wolfsburg. Here a four-door sedan shares the "moving road" to the rail link with a selection of 1303 Bugs. *Volkswagen (UK)*

April 1975, the LT was available in three versions: The LT28, LT31, and the LT35, the numbers indicating the laden weight of each model (i.e., 2.8 tons, 3.1 tons, or 3.5 tons). Built at the Hannover factory, the LT soon earned respect for its rugged character and good performance, due in part to the Audi 100–derived engine used in the gasoline version. A

2.7-liter diesel model was also offered, with the engine developed for VW by the British Perkins company.

Although Audi had been building the subcompact 50 model since September 1974, Volkswagen didn't release its own version, the Polo, until March the following year. With its 40-horsepower, 900-cc engine, the Polo was never exported to the United

The Scirocco was the first of the new breed of water-cooled Volkswagens to be launched, in 1974. With its transversely located engine driving the front wheels, the Giugiaro-styled sports coupé was an immediate success. *Volkswagen (UK)*

The Scirocco wasn't just a pretty face, for its hatchback design made it a very practical car. With a top speed of almost 110 miles per hour, it was no slouch, either, even though it was initially powered by a modest 1,500-cc engine.

States, but proved to be a big success on the European market, where demand for small hatchback cars was high. The Polo was joined by a notchback version, called the Derby, in February 1977.

GOLF GTI—A HIT FROM THE START

The most exciting news of the decade, though, had to be the launch in September 1975 of the amazing Golf GTI, a high-performance version of the Golf powered by a 110-horsepower 1.6-liter engine. The GTI was a hit from the start, receiving a rapturous welcome from the motoring press who saw it as marking the end of the line for traditional sports cars.

With its genuine top speed of 112 miles per hour, a 0-to-60-mile-per-hour time of under nine seconds, and handling equally impressive, the Golf GTI turned the world of performance cars on its head.

The Golf GTI was followed in June 1976 by a similarly powered Scirocco GTI. This Scirocco was slightly faster due to better aerodynamics and, according to Volkswagen, was quicker off the mark, too. But to everyone else, the Scirocco felt a little more ponderous than the Golf version, which remained the sporting driver's favorite.

The Golf really made its mark on the world and, just two years after its launch, the 1,000,000th example rolled off the line. To cope with demand across the Atlantic, Volkswagen announced plans to build an assembly plant in the United States, in Westmoreland, Pennsylvania, where Rabbits were produced for the domestic market, beginning in April 1978.

The sporting Golf was joined by a far more pedestrian model in September 1976 when the Golf Diesel was launched. Much of its success could be attributed to the rising price of crude oil on the world market, which, in turn, brought about a rise in gas prices. Not a glamorous car, the Golf Diesel was, nevertheless, agile and fun to drive. It was joined in August 1978, by the Passat Diesel and then new diesel versions of the LT, which used Volkswagen's own six-cylinder engine.

The Scirocco soon found its way onto the race track, where its agile handling made it a winner. Note the rear spoiler—a factory-fitted extra on performance models.

The ultimate Scirocco was the Storm, a special edition with full leather interior and a 110-horsepower fuel-injected engine. Storm models have become sought after by enthusiasts.

This is the car that really changed the face of Volkswagen: the VW Golf. Built on the same floorpan as the Scirocco, the Golf was available in both two- and four-door versions. It soon became the benchmark for all compact hatchbacks.

The Golf looked its best in two-door format. Note the heavier rear C-pillars—these have remained a Golf trademark to this day. Small chrome-plated bumpers soon gave way to heavier plastic-covered items.

In the United States, the Golf was sold as the Rabbit, a name which was supposed to reflect its agility and fun-loving nature. U.S. safety laws required the use of heavier bumpers.

The big news for 1978 was that, on January 19, Beetle production in Europe finally came to an end. Future examples sold on the domestic market–other than the cabriolets which were still built by Karmann in Osnabrück–would be shipped over from Mexico. It was indeed the end of an era.

Production of a new military vehicle called the Iltis was started in November 1978. Based on the Auto-Union Munga, another military vehicle powered by a two-stroke engine, the Iltis used the drivetrain of the Passat, with modifications to allow four-wheel drive. This no-nonsense machine proved very successful and was used extensively by the German and NATO armed forces.

But what of the trusty VW Transporter? Following its redesign for the 1968 model year, the so-called "bay-window" model remained in production with only detail changes (a new Type 4–based engine in 1974, for example) to its specification. All this was to change in May 1979, when the Type 25 was announced. This was a new Transporter with coil-spring suspension and very angular styling. Known in the United States as the Vanagon, the Type 25 was still powered by a rear-mounted air-cooled engine, but that was about the only similarity to its predecessor.

The final new faces to appear were a stylish cabriolet version of the Golf–complete with Karmann-built bodywork–and the Jetta, a notchback version of the popular Golf for those who preferred their cars with a separate trunk rather than a hatchback. Never a visually exciting car, the Jetta would ultimately prove to be more popular in the United States than the Golf, though the opposite was true in Europe. At the top of the line was the Jetta GTI.

Europe of the 1970s had seen some dramatic changes in the VW line-up, with several new models, water-cooling, and a farewell to some familiar faces. In South America, Volkswagen sales were strong and there were several models in production that were unique to the market. Cars like the Brasilia and the Variant II, the sporting SP, and the domestically produced Passat all sold well alongside the Beetle, the success of which showed no signs of waning. Volkswagen may have begun the decade on unsteady feet but, by the end of the 1970s, it was ready to take on all comers.

To meet federal laws, the U.S.-specification models were required to run small side-marker lights. Despite these, and the larger bumpers, the Rabbit still managed to look very stylish.

The large glass area gave the Golf/Rabbit a light and airy feel to the interior. The hatchback meant that it was possible to carry quite large loads with ease. A true design classic if ever there was one.

The Golf was even built in Mexico, where it was renamed the Caribe. Note the unique taillight treatment and the U.S.-spec bumpers.

The Golf GL, shown here, was joined by the Golf GLS—both high-specification models with plenty of extras, such as a steel sunroof, higher level of trim, and tinted glass. *Volkswagen (UK)*

The Golf was a real hit on the race tracks. Its light weight and agile handling made it more than a match for far more powerful opposition.

In rallying, too, the Golf soon proved itself a success. Its rugged construction and unburstable engine won it many friends.

In 1979, Volkswagen used the Golf as the basis for the IRVW 1, a vehicle designed to explore fuel-efficiency and passenger safety. Note the rubber surround to the front end.

What, no gasoline? The 1978 Golf-Elektro was an electric-powered experimental vehicle, built at a time when every manufacturer was thinking about alternatives to fossil fuels.

In April 1975, the Volkswagen commercial vehicle range expanded into a whole new market with the launch of the LT models. Built at the Hannover factory, the LTs proved to be a great success.

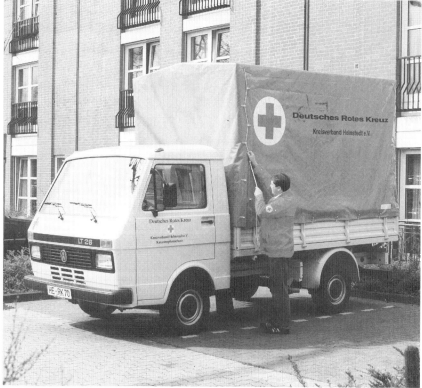

The LT was available in a wide variety of styles, including a useful pickup. This example was used by the German Red Cross for aid work. The LT28 badging shows it had a payload of 2.8 tons.

This is Volkswagen's line-up of commercial vehicles in 1975, which included a fire truck (left), an ambulance (top left), and a police vehicle (top center). Few other manufacturers could match this range.

Developed in the early 1970s for use in Third World countries, the Type 200ME Muli was a simple and inexpensive utility vehicle, which was built in Mexico and exported CKD (Completely Knocked Down or fully disassembled). It used components from the Beetle, the K70, and the Type 2.

Another version of the Type 200ME, known as the Hormiga. Note the slightly different design of the cab and the later-style Type 2 wheels, compared with the Muli.

In March 1975, Volkswagen released the Polo, a subcompact hatchback based on the Audi 50 model. The styling was clearly a reflection of the contemporary Scirocco. *Volkswagen (UK)*

While the base-model Polo came with a little 900-cc engine, the top-of-the-line GLS model was fitted with a more powerful 1,100-cc unit. Front-end styling was clearly influenced by the experimental IRVW 1. *Volkswagen (UK)*

February 1977 saw the launch of the Derby, a notchback ("three-box") version of the Polo. Its styling was intended to appeal to the more conservative purchaser.

The Derby, like the Polo, was never sold in North America, where there was little demand for small subcompacts. In Europe, the Polo far outsold the Derby. *Volkswagen (UK)*

The hottest news in 1975 was the launch of the Golf GTI—a 110-horsepower, fuel-injected Golf that rewrote the book on small performance cars. The GTI offered superb performance and handling, all wrapped up in a practical hatchback body shell. *Volkswagen (UK)*

Initially only available in left-hand drive, the GTI was eventually made available with the steering wheel on the right for the United Kingdom market. Here, a 1979 model displays typical three-wheeling Golf cornering antics. *Volkswagen (UK)*

In 1978, Beetle production finally came to an end in Europe, causing many a tear to be shed among the Wolfsburg workforce. However, new models continued to be sold, shipped all the way from Mexico.

The Iltis was conceived as an all-wheel-drive military vehicle, in the style of the old Willys Jeep. Developed from the two-stroke-powered Auto Union Munga, it used the 1,700-cc, four-cylinder, water-cooled engine from the Passat.

Although the Iltis was intended as a military vehicle first and foremost, Volkswagen recognized that there was a civilian market for such a rugged vehicle. Unfortunately, its high price meant that sales were disappointing.

The Iltis was even raced—in 1980, two German and two French teams used specially adapted examples to tackle the infamous Paris-Dakar desert endurance event.

By the mid-1970s, Volkswagen's passenger car range looked like this, with water-cooled models such as the Golf, Scirocco, and Passat sharing space in the dealerships with the old air-cooled Beetle sedan and cabriolet. The only models missing in this line-up are the Polo and Derby.

In May 1979, the Type 2 underwent a major revision, to reappear as the Type 25. The angular styling took a little getting used to, but everyone seemed to appreciate the new coil-spring suspension and superior carrying capacity.

The larger rear hatch and sliding side door made loading the Type 25 very easy. The example shown here is in fact a preproduction prototype known as the EA162, photographed just a month before the final version went into production.

The Type 25 was every bit as versatile as its predecessor—the pickup, for example, still came with useful side storage lockers. A double-cab version also formed part of the line-up.

The German postal service (*Deutsche Bundespost*) immediately bought a whole fleet of the new Transporters for its use. Painted bright yellow, they soon became a common sight on German roads.

The Jetta was launched in 1979 as an alternative to the Golf. It was a more traditional notchback design and came in a variety of models. This is the top-of-the-line Jetta GLI, the equivalent of the Golf GTI and powered by the same 110-horsepower engine. *Volkswagen (UK)*

The Jetta was quite a lot longer than the Golf, with a longer nose and greater rear overhang. Although in most people's eyes it lacked the style of its hatchback stablemate, the Jetta proved popular in the United States.

The Karmann-built Golf cabriolet was a stylish and practical alternative to a traditional sports car. In typical Karmann fashion, the top was so well made that, with the roof up, the cabriolet was as quiet as the sedan model.

In South America, Volkswagen's factories did their own thing, producing unique models for the domestic market. This is the Brasilia, a compact hatchback launched in 1973. It was initially built solely in Brazil but a year later the Mexican factory began assembly of the model.

The Brasilia was available in both two-door and four-door body styles. From this angle the similarity to the Type 4 Variant (Wagon) is plain to see.

The Mexican-built Variant II was another South America-only product.

This VW 1500 was essentially a Brazilian four-door Type 3 Fastback, a model which was never built in Europe. Styling was unusual, to say the least!

There was even a locally built Karmann-Ghia—note the unique wheels and bumper on the Brazilian version.

The Brazilian VW SP2 was a fiberglass-bodied sports car, reputedly designed by Rudolph Leiding, VW's boss in the 1970s. Powered by a 1,700-cc Type 4 engine, it proved very popular.

The Mexican factory continued to turn out Beetles in the thousands and often struggled to keep up with local demand. While the popularity of the Beetle may have waned in Europe, the South Americans couldn't get enough of them.

The year was 1972 and, long after the old split-windshield Transporter had disappeared from European and North American dealers, the Brazilian factory continued to build this out-dated model.

Volkswagen spent a lot of time and money exploring the concept of a subcompact city car. This was the first prototype to bear the name Chico (also written as "Chicco"), and dates back to 1975. Over one foot shorter than the Polo, it was still able to seat four adults in reasonable comfort.

The Brazilian line-up for 1979 included locally built Passats, Brasilias, Beetles, and, finally, the second-generation Transporter.

CHAPTER SEVEN

1980–1989:
A Thoroughly Modern Company

The 1980s began on a high for Volkswagen, with many excellent models in its line-up, but it was no time for complacency. Despite the success, for example, of the original Passat, Volkswagen announced a revised model in October 1980. More elegant and spacious, the second-generation Passat was offered with a wider variety of options than its predecessor. Everything from a tiny (for a vehicle of this size) 1.3-liter four-cylinder to a 2.2-liter five-cylinder engine was available. Diesel models also

formed part of the line-up and, in 1984, VW even launched a four-wheel-drive Synchro model.

The Passat wasn't the only model to get a facelift, for March 1981 saw the release of the Mark 2 version of the Scirocco. With a body designed in-house by VW stylists, the new-look sports coupé was available with 1.3-, 1.6-, and 1.8-liter engines, including the impressive fuel-injected engine of the Golf GTI. Its styling was more rounded than that of the original Scirocco and took a while to be accepted. Somehow it

The new decade began on a high, with the launch of a new Passat range. The updated model looked far more stylish than its predecessor and offered higher levels of trim.

The second-generation Passat took the image of Volkswagen one step closer to that of its sister company, Audi, which had always been perceived slightly more exclusive. The Passat Wagon made an impressive load carrier.

had lost the crisp lines of the original, although it still retained the Mark 1 Golf's floorpan and drivetrain.

Following the success of the Passat, with its fastback and wagon body styles, Volkswagen tried its hand at a midsized "three-box" sedan in the form of the Santana. Launched in September 1981, this was essentially a redesigned Passat. Unfortunately, even though this was a worthy car, with all of its forebear's mechanical attributes, the Santana was something of a disappointment in sales. VW only managed to sell 198,000 of these before production ceased in 1985.

Volkswagen was clearly refusing to rest on its laurels and launched a new Polo in 1981, followed by the Derby in February 1982. The latter was a simple sedan with a separate trunk, which, while not the most exciting of vehicles, was a popular addition to

the range. But that was not all, for a coupé version of the Polo was launched in September 1982, to complete the line-up.

THE BEETLE SOLDIERS ON

Sadly, the much-loved Beetle cabriolet, still built in Germany by Karmann, finally reached the end of the road in January 1980. However, there was still life in the old Beetle sedan, which set another production record on May 15, 1981, when the 20,000,000th example left the assembly line, this time in Puebla, Mexico. To celebrate, a special edition, called the Silver Bug, was offered. It was joined in the spring of 1982 by the fun Jeans Bug, complete with denim-trimmed interior and bright yellow, red, or white paintwork.

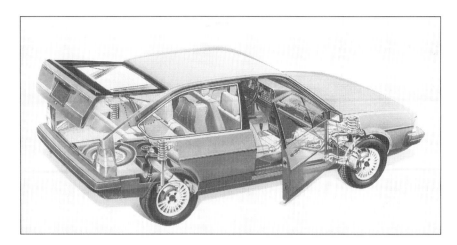

In North America, the revised Passat was sold as the Quantum in an effort to distance it from the old Dasher. This ghosted view shows the basic fastback model.

The Mark 2 Scirocco was launched in September 1981 and was offered with 1.3-, 1.6-, and 1.8-liter engines. Top of the range was the fuel-injected GTI model, seen here leading the line-up.

The VW Santana was a conventional three-box sedan derived from the Passat. It was a well-equipped car but not the most successful model in Volkswagen's range.

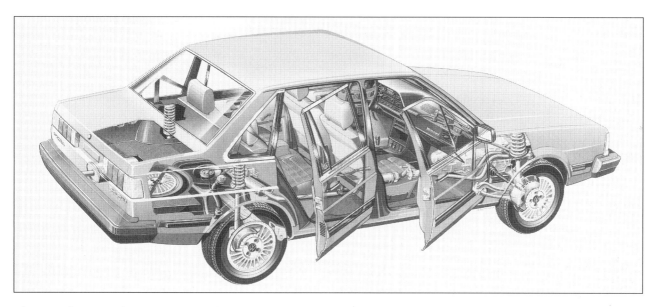

The United States–only Quantum was also produced as a conventional four-door sedan, just like the Santana. Larger "federal" bumpers helped distinguish the Quantum from the Santana.

In 1981, Volkswagen released the second-generation Polo. It was initially launched as a hatchback, with a wagonlike body, but the following year a stylish coupé was added to the range.

There was plenty else happening in South America, too, with models such as the Gol—a small Polo-sized sedan powered by a front-mounted, air-cooled engine derived from that of the Beetle—and the Voyage and Parati. The Voyage was a two- or four-door sedan powered by the engine from the Brazilian version of the Passat. Designed to run on alcohol rather than regular gasoline, the Voyage was joined in the show room by the Parati, a station wagon version. In a similar vein was the Argentinian-built

In 1987, Volkswagen used the Polo as a test bed for a new city-car project. The result was the OKO-Polo, a frugal runabout powered by a tiny, two-cylinder diesel engine. However, it never went into production.

Shortly after the new Polo was announced, Volkswagen introduced an updated Derby. The addition of a separate trunk did little to enhance the Polo's lines. However, the Derby proved popular with a more conservative market.

Gacel, another midsized sedan, the Corsar (another Passat derivative), and the Atlantic (Jetta), both of which were built in Mexico. None of these models was sold outside South America, but they were popular in their respective domestic markets.

One South American model that was exported to North America and Canada between 1987 and 1990 was the Fox. This was available in three different body styles: two-door sedan, four-door sedan, and a two-door wagon. Although not the most groundbreaking design, the Fox still has a loyal band of followers to this day. There was also the Saveiro, a pickup version of the Gol, also powered by a front-mounted Beetle engine. None of these cars was based on the chassis of any existing European model and served to show how independently of the German headquarters the South American factories were allowed to operate.

In June 1982, Volkswagen further expanded its overseas interests by signing an agreement with the Chinese-owned Shanghai Tractor and Automobile Corporation. This agreement would lead to the assembly of the VW in China for sales on the

The Beetle continued to sell well in South America and was still exported to Europe in considerable numbers. By now, little further development work was being carried out, the body style having remained virtually unchanged since 1968.

On May 15, 1981, the 20,000,000th Beetle left the assembly line at Puebla, Mexico. To celebrate this momentous occasion, a special model called the Silver Bug was offered for sale.

domestic market. The first vehicle built under this arrangement was completed on April 11, 1983. In fact, the Chinese factory continued to use the Santana name long after 1985, when it had been dropped in Germany.

For Volkswagen in Germany, the Golf was still the number one seller. However, by 1983, it had been in production and relatively unchanged for nine years. In August 1983, Volkswagen released the second-generation Golf, and at the same time aban-

doned the name Rabbit in the North American market. Built on a new, longer-wheelbase floorpan, it won universal praise from the motoring press for its greater level of refinement. It was joined soon after by the second-generation Jetta, a car that was to prove extremely popular in North America, more so, in fact, than the Golf. Once again, the reverse was true in Europe.

Both the Golf and Jetta were offered in a wide variety of models, including high-performance 16-valve

The VW Gol (not Golf!) was a Brazilian-built compact powered by a front-mounted Beetle engine driving the front wheels. Its styling was reminiscent of the Polo's, but it was also clearly influenced by the Mark 1 Scirocco.

From the rear, the similarity between the Gol and the original Scirocco is plain to see. Hatchback design made the Gol a practical car—the Beetle-based engine gave it traditional VW reliability.

The Voyage was a Brazilian-built sedan, available with two or four doors. It was powered by the same engine as the locally built Passat and exported to North America as the Fox. It clearly made quite a splash when it was first launched.

The Parati—the wagon version of the Voyage—was also sent north of the border as the Fox wagon. This proved a popular model, offering versatility and value for the money.

The VW Fox sedan was an unglamorous model, but helped fill a gap in Volkswagen's North American line-up. Wheels shown are the same as fitted to early Golf and Scirocco models in Europe.

GTI versions and turbo diesels. There was even a G60 supercharged Golf and two four-wheel-drive synchro models, called the Golf Country and the G60 Rallye. Interestingly, the Golf cabriolet continued in production virtually unchanged, still based on the Mark 1 model and built by the Karmann factory in Germany. In fact, there never was a Mark 2 Golf-based cabriolet.

The trusty Beetle, which had been imported from Mexico since 1978, finally disappeared from European show rooms after the last boatload arrived at Emden on August 12, 1985. There was much public uproar about this, but, as Volkswagen tried hard to explain, there was little chance of the Beetle meeting strict European emissions regulations without considerable investment on the manufacturer's part. As sales were relatively modest, such expenditure did not make sense. However, it didn't take long for private imports to begin, with a number of independent German dealers offering their own catalytic converter conversions. The Beetle simply refused to die.

The Corsar was a Mexican-built, mid-sized sedan based on the Passat. It was a well-equipped model with a high level of trim. However, it was never sold outside South America.

The Volkswagen Atlantic was a Mexican-built Jetta. Note the dual rectangular headlights, which set it apart from the European models. Again, this was never sold outside South America.

In April 1985, the third-generation Passat was announced, its styling causing much interest as there was no radiator grille at the front of the vehicle. Instead, air was ducted into the engine bay from beneath the front bumper. This new model was offered only in sedan and Variant (wagon) styles—there was no longer the option of a fastback body style.

The big news for sporting drivers was the arrival of the new Karmann-assembled Corrado coupe in the fall of 1988. This stylish two-plus-two was built in a similar vein to the aging Scirocco, which had been in production in one style or another since 1974. The Corrado was powered by either the 16-valve or supercharged G60 Golf engines, both of which resulted in more than adequate performance, but it was criticized for being too expensive and lacking in passenger space. The Corrado is often referred to as a replacement for the Scirocco but, in fact, this is not strictly true, for the Mark 2 Scirocco continued in production for more than two years after the introduction of the Corrado.

Throughout the 1980s, Volkswagen was constantly looking toward the future—not just the next two or three years, but right into the next century.

The Caribe was the Mexican-built Golf for the domestic market. It was available as a two- or four-door model. The small square headlights were unique to this version of Golf.

Several prototypes were built to give a glimpse of what the future might hold for Volkswagen's customers around the world, both in terms of styling and technology. In 1980, VW built the Aerodynamic Research Volkswagen (ARVW), a record-attempt vehicle with a six-cylinder diesel engine. It reached a top speed of over 360 kilometers (223 miles) per hour. Also developed in 1980 was the IRVW 2 (Integrated Research Volkswagen). Loosely based on the Passat, it was an exercise in fuel-saving aerodynamics and passenger safety.

Then, in 1981, a rather slab-sided concept car was shown at the IAA Motor Show in Frankfurt. Powered by a three-cylinder diesel engine, it was called the Auto 2000. Several of its styling details would later resurface on the third-generation Passat.

STUDENT, POLO SPRINT, TWIN-ENGINED SCIROCCO

In 1982 came the Student—a small city car with impact-absorbing plastic bumpers and a cheeky look. Later came the Polo Sprint, a whimsical mid-engined Polo powered by a high-performance, flat-four, air-cooled engine where the rear seats should be. It was accompanied by an equally potent twin-engined Scirocco. Twice the power and four-wheel drive could have made this a serious rally contender, had Volkswagen decided to pursue the idea.

There was also the Scooter, a three-wheeled fun car and the much more strait-laced IRVW 3, based on the Jetta, which was a design exercise to create a safe, ecologically friendly sedan. Finally came the IRVW Futura, with its radical gullwing doors and "one-box" styling. Everybody thought it unlikely anything like that would ever see production—but, gullwing doors aside, doesn't it look uncannily like the dozens of MPVs we see on our roads today?

If the 1980s was a decade full of surprises, just wait and see what the 1990s (and beyond) offer.

From the rear, the Caribe was virtually indistinguishable from the European Golf. Only the badging and side reflectors suggest that this is anything other than a regular Golf GL four-door.

The Saveiro was a practical small pickup based on the Gol. The engine was still the Beetle-derived unit mounted at the front and driving the front wheels.

A pickup version of the Golf, called the Caddy in Europe, was launched and sold very well. There was even a high-performance model powered by the Golf GTI engine, called the Caddy Sport.

In 1983, Volkswagen announced that the original Golf was about to be replaced—by another Golf. The second-generation or Mark 2 Golf was a hit from the start. This is a U.S.-specification GTI model, with characteristic rectangular headlights. European models had four round lights.

The Jetta was updated at the same time across all markets. This is actually a Mexican-built example but it is virtually indistinguishable from its European equivalent.

Following an agreement between the Shanghai Tractor and Automobile Corporation and Volkswagen in 1984, VW Santanas were built under the Shanghai name in China.

Top of the range was the Jetta GT 16v. This had the same powerful 16-valve fuel-injected engine used in the Golf GTI 16v. Volkswagen claimed a 130-mile-per-hour top speed for this model. *Volkswagen (UK)*

In the United States, the Jetta was a big hit, outselling the Golf by two-to-one. It seems that Americans preferred a trunk to a hatchback, despite the obvious advantages of the latter.

There were three four-wheel drive versions of the Golf. The first, the Golf Synchro, looked little different to the regular Golf, but the Golf Country wore full off-road equipment, while the Golf Rallye was powered by the supercharged G60 engine. It was built for Volkswagen by Steyr.

Volkswagen continued to examine alternative power sources for its cars. This is the Golf Elektro-Hybrid, which was equipped with a small diesel engine and an electric motor for use in towns.

The OKO-Golf was fitted with a catalytic converter and a special automatic transmission. It was among the first diesels to be fitted with a catalyst.

On August 12, 1985, the last Beetle destined for Germany left the Mexican factory. The sign reads: "The last Mexican Beetle produced for Germany. From Mexico with love."

In April 1985, the third-generation Passat was released, its styling provoking much comment due to the lack of a conventional radiator grille. Air was ducted into the engine bay from below the front bumper.

Even though the Mark 2 Scirocco was selling steadily, there were plans afoot to build another sports coupe. This styling sketch was for a project that ultimately resulted in the Corrado.

The Karmann-built Corrado was a very stylish coupé. It was offered with three engine options: the 16v Golf engine, the super-charged G60 unit, or, later in its life, the silky-smooth VR6.

Volkswagen's range of light commercial vehicles was pretty impressive by the mid-1980s, with no fewer than 10 Type 25 models and two Caddies. The Type 25 line-up included emergency vehicles, a taxi, and two pickups.

The double-cab pickup (or crew cab, as it was often known) was very popular in the United States. This is a water-cooled model, distinguishable by the two grilles on the front panel.

Even though Europe had long abandoned both the split-windshield and bay-window Type 2s in favor of the Type 25, the Brazilian factory continued to produce its own amalgamation of the two old designs. The cab is from a second-generation Transporter, the rest is almost pure split-windshield style. Bizarre.

From the rear, the Brazilian bus presents a confusing sight to anyone used to European or North American models: Late-style taillights and wheels, yet early-style air vents, rear hatch, and pop-out side windows. Note, too, the rear quarter-windows, which are similar to those fitted to the original Deluxe bus of the 1950s.

The 1980 ARVW (as in Aerodynamic Research Volkswagen) was a vehicle built to break records. Powered by a 2,383-cc turbo diesel engine, it was capable of well over 200 miles per hour.

The IRVW 2 (Integrated Research Volkswagen) was based on the contemporary Passat and was built as an exercise in aerodynamics and passenger safety.

The Auto 2000 was powered by a three-cylinder diesel engine. It was designed to look at ways to improve fuel-efficiency. Weighing just 750 kilograms (1,650 pounds), the Auto 2000 could reach almost 95 miles per hour and yet return around 60 miles per gallon.

The 1,100-cc Student was built in 1982 as part of a program to develop a small city car. Using the engine and drivetrain from the Polo, the Student remained another unrealized dream.

There were several twin-engined Sciroccos. They were built to examine the possibility of using dual-engine technology in competition. Sadly, the concept never made it past the prototype stage.

The strange Scooter was a fun, three-wheeled sports car, which again never made it into production. Gullwing doors may look cool, but they can be a problem in crowded parking lots!

The Polo Sprint may look simply like a customized Polo hatchback, but it sported a 156-horsepower flat-four engine, placed where you would normally expect the rear seat to be. It remained a one-off.

The Scooter remains an exciting concept. Who knows, with our roads getting ever more crowded, Volkswagen might one day dust off the prototype and build it for real.

Far more down to earth was the IRVW 3, a Jetta-based safety vehicle with run-flat tires and antilock braking system. Many of its features would reappear years later on production models.

The amazing IRVW Futura was a very attractive "one-box" design that isn't too unlike many of today's smaller MPVs. The vast glass area would have required full-time air conditioning!

The Futura also came with gullwing doors, a popular design feature in the late 1980s. Isn't it a shame that this stunning creation never made it into the dealerships and out onto our roads?

The EA276 may not look beautiful, but it was a serious test bed for a future small car. The drivetrain appears to be Golf (the wheels are from the Mark 1 Golf GTI or GLS).

Although Karmann built the prototype, the Jetta cabriolet never made it into production, either. Like the Golf cabriolet, this Jetta featured a built-in rollover bar for added passenger safety.

The Orbit was another stillborn project. Many of its features, though, were carried through to the Passat and beyond. The front-end styling, for example, was very reminiscent of the third-generation Passat.

CHAPTER EIGHT

1990s and Beyond: Volkswagen Looks to the Future

With such an action-packed decade in the 1980s, it was hard to see how Volkswagen could continue at such a rate of progress toward the twenty-first century. But times were changing and customer expectations were high. Volkswagen's line-up was under pressure from Far Eastern products, which by now were a match for the best that Europe could offer, both in quality and specification.

The decade began with a new look for two old favorites: the Polo and the Transporter. To be fair, the Polo's revision was largely cosmetic, with a new sloping front and consequently much-improved aerodynamics. There was also a larger range of engine options, including a supercharged version, the G40–the ultimate factory "hot hatchback," to use a popular expression.

The Transporter, on the other hand, came in for a total redesign. Gone was the rear-mounted engine (which, since 1982, had been water-cooled anyway) and the angular styling, first seen back in May 1979. The new model, called the T4, was a thoroughly modern design, with a front-mounted engine driving the front wheels. This drive layout allowed the designers to locate the rear floor as low as possible to facilitate loading, just like the original Transporter. Many rival commercial vehicles had to accommodate prop-shafts and rear axles, causing the load area to be several inches higher.

The T4 was a hit from the word "go," with several different versions on offer, ranging from vans to pickups, campers to executive transporters. Although the T4 may not have had much in common with its predecessors in technical terms, it continued the tradition of versatility that had made the original Type 2 such a success.

In 1991, the Volkswagen Golf, still very much the mainstay of the range, was re-released in Mark 3 form.

Fans of the Volkswagen Transporter were in for a real shock when Volkswagen announced it was dropping the traditional rear-engined design in favor of the ultramodern, front-engined, front-wheel-drive T4!

The new model was quite unlike any previous Transporter but has proved to be every bit as versatile. Shown here is a special limited-edition model, launched in the year 2000 to celebrate 50 years of the world's favorite commercial vehicle. *Volkswagen (UK)*

The new model continued the styling tradition of heavy rear C-pillars, which had been part of the distinctive original 1974 design, but was thoroughly up-to-date in all other respects. For some enthusiasts' tastes, the Mark 3 Golf was too clumsy in its appearance, a

The T4 was also available as an executive MPV called the Caravelle Limousine. Powered by the superb VR6 engine, this was a luxury taxi like no other! *Volkswagen (UK)*

Such was the rate of sales of the new Transporter that between its launch in 1990 and 1994, it sold over a half-million examples. This publicity vehicle shouted out the good news.

feeling further strengthened when they got behind the wheel. The new Golf was clearly heavier than the two previous models, largely due to added safety-related strengthening, and its handling suffered as a result. On the open road, though, the car felt more refined and it was certainly better equipped than any previous Golf. At last there was also a Mark 3–based cabriolet—all previous models had been based on the original Mark 1 Golf. In common with its predecessor, the new cabriolet was built by Karmann at Osnabrück.

The new Golf was offered with a wide variety of engine options, including a quite sensational six-cylinder engine, called the VR6. This narrow-angle V-6 took up little more space than a conventional four-cylinder unit, yet was blessed with enormous torque and smoothness. The same engine was used in the Corrado, where it also received favorable reviews.

The Jetta name disappeared from the Volkswagen line-up in all countries except the United States—everywhere else, the sedan version of the new Golf was called the Vento. Why? Simply because the name Jetta

In Germany, you could buy the California Club, a specially adapted T4 with all the extras you can imagine—just right for heading off to the Alpine ski slopes for Christmas.

had become synonymous with a rather underwhelming sedan that had failed to meet sales expectations—except in North America, where the Jetta outsold the Golf two-to-one! By changing the name in Europe, VW hoped that this worthy sedan would stand a better chance of survival in the show room wars. With its higher level of sophistication, or just the new name, the new Vento soon outsold its predecessor.

The early 1990s saw a growth in interest in the development of small, fuel-efficient city cars, as once again rising oil prices forced up the cost of gas, and pressure from ecologists made manufacturers think green. Volkswagen responded in 1991 by showing the Chico, a subcompact sedan that promised big-car safety. The Chico was an attractive little car and seemed destined for production when, as legend has it, the decision was made to axe the project at the 11th hour. If Volkswagen was to enter this highly competitive market, it wanted its product to be perfect. The Chico was not, at least in management's eyes.

Volkswagen wasn't averse to trying revolutionary ideas in the marketplace, proof being the launch of the Golf Ecomatic and CitySTROMer models. The Ecomatic was powered by a diesel engine that was automatically shut off each time the vehicle came to a rest, so as to save fuel and emissions. The model was dropped after less than two years. The CitySTROMer was an all-electric version, with a range of about 120 kilometers (75 miles). It, too, failed to arouse public interest.

In 1993, the worthy Passat was completely updated, bringing with it levels of refinement one might reasonably expect from cars costing far more. However, the sedan version was not a great success, being outsold two-to-one by the Variant (wagon) model. It wasn't, in fact, until 1996 that the Passat sedan came into its own, when the entirely new Passat range was launched to world acclaim. The new-look sedan was joined soon after by the wagon, for which order books were filled the moment it was announced.

Not all T4s are glamorous. This is the versatile double-cab tipper—perfect for anyone in the construction industry. Factory-approved conversion was available to order.

Another variation on the tipper theme, this time with a side-tipping body and based on a single-cab pickup.

And then there's the flatbed with a crane. Clearly the new T4 had lost none of its forebear's adaptability.

In 1991, the second-generation Golf was finally dropped from the VW line-up to make way for the third-generation model. The new car was heavier than its predecessor, largely due to added safety features.

The Mark 3 Golf GTI was initially criticized by fans of the earlier models for being overweight and slightly underpowered. However, it was considerably more refined, and it continued to sell well.

INNOVATIONS: V-5 AND TDI

The new Passats were powered by a range of engines, including an innovative V-5 motor, which was essentially a VR6 with one cylinder lopped off. Almost as powerful and torquey, the V-5 proved to be every bit as smooth as its big brother, the VR6. For many critics, though, the way ahead lay with Volkswagen's superb TDI (Turbo Diesel Injection) range of engines, which offered gasoline-engine performance and sophistication with miserly gas mileage. A perfect example of having your cake and eating it, too. As gas prices continue to rise, the fuel-efficient TDI motors will surely become the engines of choice.

But what of the Beetle in all this time? Production had ceased long ago in Germany but continued unabated in Mexico, where the sedan was still a strong seller. However, a most unlikely situation occurred in 1993, when the Brazilian government backed a scheme to start building the Fusca (Brazilian for Beetle) once again, after a lapse of almost seven years. The Beetle was refusing to lie down and die.

In fact, the whole Beetle phenomenon was about to be given a tremendous boost with the arrival on the scene of Concept 1, a styling exercise which appeared at the 1994 Detroit Auto Show. Designed by J. C. Mays and Freeman Thomas, who worked at VW's styling studio in Simi Valley, California, Concept 1 was full of visual references to the original air-cooled Volkswagen, such as separate fenders, running boards—even a dash-mounted bud vase, just like the popular accessories of the 1950s.

Finally there was a new Golf cabriolet with the arrival of the Mark 3 version. Built by Karmann (as had been the two previous VW cabriolets), the new model was a hit from the word go.

The Corrado continued in production into the 1990s, powered by either the "basic" 16v Golf engine, the supercharged G60 motor, or the awesome VR6. The six-cylinder model is a very desirable car with a big following among enthusiasts.

With the arrival of a new Golf came a new Jetta—or Vento, to give it its European name. The Jetta had never been a big seller outside North America, so it was hoped that a name change might help matters. It didn't—the Golf continued to outsell it by a considerable margin.

Concept 1 was an immediate hit with press and public alike, and their enthusiasm was further fueled with the showing of a cabriolet version at the following year's Geneva Motor Show in Switzerland. Strong public interest in such a fun, retro-styled vehicle clearly influenced Volkswagen's decision to go ahead with the project, finally announcing at the 1995 Japan Motor Show that the car would be built and that it was to be named the New Beetle—much to the disgust of some old-timers who felt the name Beetle could only be applied to the original air-cooled model.

The New Beetle was finally released in 1998, based on the floorpan of the latest Golf model and with the same front-wheel-drive drivetrain. Several versions are now in production, ranging from the basic 2-liter gasoline-engined model right up to a

powerful VR6-powered performance version, the RSi. Although the New Beetle may not have much in common with its forebear, it has succeeded in raising the profile of Volkswagen to new heights—especially in North America, the market at which it was squarely aimed.

Throughout all this time, the Golf continued to be improved, refined, and ultimately completely redesigned, appearing in 1997 in its fourth incarnation. Larger, heavier, and even better equipped, the new Golf was a far cry from the original but, thanks to clever styling details, the model's heritage could still be visually traced back to the Mark 1 of 1974. The only model that didn't benefit from a total redesign was the cabriolet, which continued in production in Mark 3 guise, albeit with a remodeled front end to reflect the Mark 4's new styling.

There was nothing wrong at all with the Vento—it was just that the European public preferred a hatchback to a three-box sedan. In the United States, the model continued to be called the Jetta and sold in considerable numbers.

The Golf CitySTROMer was another attempt at developing an environmentally friendly, fuel-saving vehicle. This electric-powered Golf was seen as a step in the right direction.

The new Golf was soon kept company in the show room by the Bora—the Jetta (or Vento) by another name. Essentially a Golf with a trunk, the Bora was aimed at the sub-Passat market, yet its levels of refinement were such that some dealers expressed concern that this slightly cheaper model might undermine the latter's excellent sales record.

With a wide variety of engine and drivetrain options—including a four-wheel-drive system referred to by Volkswagen as 4-Motion—the Golf and Bora formed the backbone of the Volkswagen range into the new Millennium.

But there was more to VW in the final years of the last century than a range of sedans and subcompacts, for the company showed two new MPVs in 1995. One, called the Noah, was a design exercise, while the second—the Sharan—was immediately destined for production. Noah was a compact MPV that explored the use of recycled materials in its construction and made available a variety of communications systems to the driver.

The 1996 model year saw Volkswagen celebrating 20 years of the GTI, with the launch of a special commemorative model. The GTI had come a long way since it first appeared back in the mid-1970s.

The Passat was revised yet again, with the appearance in 1993 of a much-improved line-up. However, of the models on offer, only the Passat Variant (Wagon) was a major success. The sedan was outsold two-to-one by its more versatile stablemate.

The Sharan, however, was a real departure for Volkswagen. It represented the fruits of a three-way liaison between VW, Seat (now owned by Volkswagen), and rival manufacturer Ford. Each was responsible for different aspects of its development, with cost being shared on a roughly equal basis. The Seat version was to be called the Alhambra, and Ford's the Galaxy. (American readers might have an altogether different image of what a Ford Galaxy looks like!) None of these models was offered outside the European market.

The Polo received a major revamp in 1994, the third generation of this popular model. With a completely new body and floorpan package, this popular subcompact was now available in four-door guise for the first time in its 19-year history. It was also extremely well equipped, with ABS (antilock braking system) and dual air bags available for the first time in such a small car. The new-look hatchback Polo was joined by a "three-box" notchback model, the Polo Classic and, in 1997, by a small wagon called the Polo Variant.

Volkswagen was proud of its diesel engine development program and, by 1995, could offer an impressive range of diesel-engined vehicles, including the stylish Golf Cabriolet with its TDI (Turbo Direct Injection) motor.

The third-generation Polo lasted until 2000, when it was updated yet again with revised styling, to bring it in line with the latest Golf model. The most exciting news, however, was the launch of the Polo GTI, powered by an amazing 1.6-liter engine producing some 125 horsepower—more than enough to put a smile on any driver's face in a car this small!

But the Polo wasn't the only subcompact in Volkswagen's impressive line-up as the new millennium dawned. Launched in the summer of 1998, the VW Lupo represented the smallest model in the range. With its appealing looks and excellent use of interior space, the Lupo soon proved popular with people seeking a stylish, well-made alternative to the many Japanese-built subcompacts on the market.

THE "3-LITER" LUPO—AND MORE

Although all Lupos are fun to drive, two models stand out above the rest—the "3-liter" Lupo and the Lupo GTI. The first is not, as the name suggests, a Lupo with a 3,000-cc engine, but a car which, when driven carefully, can consume as little as 3 liters of gas for every 100 kilometers—representing an amazing 78.6 miles per gallon! But then, for sheer undiluted fun, how about the GTI? With 125 horsepower on tap, this pocket-rocket can hit 127 miles per hour. Now that's fast!

However, we shall leave the last word to what is perhaps the ultimate Volkswagen ever built—one which is as diametrically opposed to the original People's Car concept as it could be: the Passat W-8. This executive sedan produces 275 horsepower from its innovative W-8 engine—essentially two V-4 units joined with a common crankshaft. With four-wheel drive and the option of a six-speed manual or five-speed Tiptronic automatic transmission, the Passat W-8 proves that, as far as Volkswagen technology is concerned, you ain't seen nothin' yet.

To prove that a diesel badge on the back didn't necessarily mean a slow vehicle, Volkswagen went racing with its Golf TDI in the Nürburgring 24-hour event.

Not content to go circuit racing, Volkswagen also backed a team of diesel rally cars. This is the Golf TDI of Steve Martin and Neil Thompson in the Manx Rally on the Isle of Man.

In 1996, the Passat range was updated yet again. With dramatic new styling and an exciting range of engines, the new Passat was a far cry from the Dasher and Quantum models of old. *Volkswagen (UK)*

Perhaps the most impressive vehicle in the line-up was the V-6 turbo diesel-engined wagon. With a 120-mile-per-hour top speed and excellent gas mileage, the Passat V-6 TDI was perfect for those long cross-country trips. *Volkswagen (UK)*

For the 2001 model year, the Passat was further redesigned, this time with a little more brightwork to reflect changing tastes in the model, which was slightly longer.

The V-6 TDI engine was also available in the Passat sedan, turning it into a true high-performance vehicle ready to take on the best from BMW and sister company Audi. But there was more to come . . . *Volkswagen (UK)*

The redesigned front end gives the Passat a more purposeful look. Chrome trim around the grille and along the bumpers adds an extra touch of class to an already very classy vehicle.

The original Beetle continued to sell steadily in South America, and its future seemed secure when, in 1993, the Brazilian government backed a scheme to recommend manufacture of the Fusca (as the Beetle is known in Brazil) after a seven-year lapse. Sadly, it disappeared again a few years later, leaving all Beetle production to Mexico. *Volkswagen do Brazil*

At the 1994 Detroit Auto Show, Volkswagen caused more than a few jaws to drop when it showed off its latest styling exercise, called Concept 1. This cute little car was full of visual references to the original Beetle.

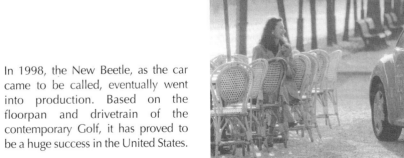

In 1998, the New Beetle, as the car came to be called, eventually went into production. Based on the floorpan and drivetrain of the contemporary Golf, it has proved to be a huge success in the United States.

A right-hand-drive version of the New Beetle was eventually produced for sale in markets such as Great Britain, Japan, Australia, and South Africa, where cars drive on the left side of the road. *Volkswagen (UK)*

However, for the ultimate wild ride, get behind the wheel of the six-cylinder, six-speed New Beetle RSi; 225 horsepower and a 140-mile-per-hour top speed turn the New Beetle into a true high-performance car.

In 1997, the venerable Golf was completely revised yet again, making this the fourth generation of the most popular water-cooled Volkswagen ever. Its floorpan is shared by the New Beetle and the Audi TT. *Volkswagen (UK)*

The new Golf is offered in a wide variety of models, including one with the impressive V-5 engine. Slightly flared fenders and large-diameter aluminum wheels give the new Golf an aggressive stance. *Volkswagen (UK)*

To keep the link with the original Golf of 1974, VW's stylists gave the Mark 4 Golf heavy C-pillars—a feature which has been common to all Golf models throughout the years. *Volkswagen (UK)*

The cabriolet appeared with revised styling to match the rest of the Mark 4 Golf range—but don't be fooled, for it's really a Mark 3 with new front-end sheet metal. *Volkswagen (UK)*

Another newcomer was the Mark 4 Golf Variant (Wagon), which offered almost as much carrying capacity as most of the older Passat wagons. In Europe, especially, midsized wagons are very popular. *Volkswagen (UK)*

In the United States, the Jetta name simply refuses to die, but in Europe the Mark 4 "Golf-with-a-trunk" is known as the Bora. With styling reminiscent of the Passat, the Bora is a very refined vehicle.

The Bora's front-end styling is more aggressive than that of the equivalent Golf, giving it a greater "presence" on the road. *Volkswagen (UK)*

In 1995, Volkswagen showed the world a styling exercise code-named Noah. The intention was to explore the use of recycled materials in vehicle manufacturing.

Noah was a simple, "one-box" design not unlike Audi's later A2 mini-MPV. Once again, gullwing doors formed part of the design, just like the Futura of the late 1980s.

The year 1995 also saw the launch of the Sharan, the result of a three-way tie-up between VW, Seat, and Ford. This stylish MPV was never sold in North America, but it proved a strong seller in Europe. *Volkswagen (UK)*

The Sharan was offered with a wide range of engine options, including a VR6 and the impressive 1.8T turbo motor. Revised styling in 2000 brought it right up-to-date.

As one has come to expect from Volkswagen, the Sharan could be ordered in any one of a number of guises, such as this emergency paramedic ambulance, or *Notarzt*, as it is called in Germany.

The Polo underwent a couple of major revisions in the final decade of the twentieth century, the 1994 update being perhaps the most striking. The popular subcompact became a worthy kid brother to the larger Golf. Volkswagen (UK)

Several special edition Polos were released, including the Open Air, a two-door model with full-length sliding sunroof and color-coded turn signal lenses. Volkswagen (UK)

Not to be left out of the wagon line-up, the Polo Variant fulfilled the needs of people wanting a small wagon that combined excellent load-carrying capacity with frugal gas mileage. Volkswagen (UK)

The Polo line-up was spearheaded by the rapid Polo GTI. Powered by a 125-horsepower fuel-injected engine, the GTI was hailed as the true successor to the original 1976 Golf GTI.

The Caddy name was resurrected in 1999 for a small delivery van based on the contemporary Polo. It soon proved to be a hit with inner-city delivery drivers, who appreciated its agile handling and compact dimensions.

With European roads becoming more crowded by the day, there has been a shift toward developing smaller subcompacts. The Lupo is Volkswagen's answer to the challenge. This is the sporty, 1.4-liter, 16-valve model. *Volkswagen (UK)*

For real rip-roaring performance, there is no substitute for the rocketlike Lupo GTI, with its 125-horsepower engine from the Polo GTI. The ultimate wolf in sheep's clothing!

At the other end of the scale is the Lupo "3-liter" TDI. No, it's not powered by a 3,000-cc engine but, instead, drinks less than 3 liters of fuel for every 100 kilometers—that's over 75 miles per gallon!

In 2001, the Polo was redesigned yet again, with styling that resembled that of the Lupo. Better equipped and more refined, the new Polo looks set for a long and happy future.

The rear-end styling is very reminiscent of the Mark 4 Golf, with its flared fenders and protruding rear bumper.

The new Passat W-8 represents the latest development in engine technology, with an innovative W engine comprising two narrow-angle V-4 units sharing a common crankshaft.

As for the trusty VW Microbus, who knows what the future holds. Following the success of the retrostyled New Beetle, Volkswagen showed this modern interpretation of the world's favorite MPV. Place your orders now . . .

INDEX

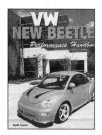

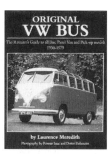